# BACKROADS & BYWAYS OF
# MINNESOTA

# BACKROADS & BYWAYS OF
# MINNESOTA

Drives, Daytrips
& Weekend Excursions

Amy C. Rea

The Countryman Press
Woodstock, Vermont

**We welcome your comments and suggestions.**

Please contact

Editor
The Countryman Press
P.O. Box 748
Woodstock, VT 05091
or e-mail countrymanpress@wwnorton.com.

Backroads & Byways of Minnesota
ISBN 978-0-88150-932-8

Interior photographs by the author unless otherwise specified
Map by Erin Greb Cartography, © The Countryman Press
Book design by Hespenheide Design
Composition by Eugenie S. Delaney

Published by The Countryman Press, P.O. Box 748, Woodstock, VT 05091

Distributed by W. W. Norton & Company, Inc., 500 Fifth Avenue, New York, NY 10110

Printed in the United States of America

10 9 8 7 6 5 4 3 2 1

*For Melissa Hanson and Carrie Stolar, my friends at
the Säjai Foundation, for their enthusiasm, encouragement,
and support for this project. Not to mention their inexhaustible
patience (though I seemed to try my hardest to exhaust it).*

# Acknowledgments

Where to even begin? So many people, directly and indirectly, helped me with this project, and in some cases I don't even know their names. For example: the blond woman at the International Falls Visitors Center who took one look at me—when I'd been on the road for hours on a hot day and had just emerged from the detour from hell—wagged her finger, and said, "You look like you could use a view and a drink." Truer words were never spoken, and her recommendation that I head east out of International Falls and make my way to Sha Sha Resort was spot on. An hour later, I was on a sunny deck overlooking Rainy Lake, enjoying a walleye salad and a Summit beer, and the stress of the day was melting away. Whoever you are, friendly woman in International Falls—thank you.

Visitors centers, chambers of commerce, servers in restaurants, clerks in stores and gas stations. Other tourists on hiking trails. Employees and volunteers at county and state historical society branches and sites. DNR folks at state parks and online. My friends on Twitter, who not only encouraged me, but gave me tips and leads (I'm talking to you, @minnemom). Kate Havelin, whose books on hiking and running inspired me to check out some state parks I might have bypassed otherwise. These are just a few of the people who gave me insight and help when I most needed it.

My thanks to Lisa Sacks at Countryman Press, for not pulling her hair out over me (as far as I know!), and for Rosalie Wieder, for her wonderfully detailed editing. (Rosalie, I promise someday to diligently study the rules of usage regarding *which* and *that*.)

My parents, Dora and Ernie Crippen, have been nothing but enthusiastic about this work and frequently provided a place to stay and early morning breakfasts while I was on the road. A day that starts with homemade buttermilk pancakes is bound to be a good one.

And, of course, Jim and Mitchell and Michael, my very own family, who coped with long absences and an exhausted wife/mother with no complaints. Well, except for having to always walk the dog. But I can live with that. Love you all!

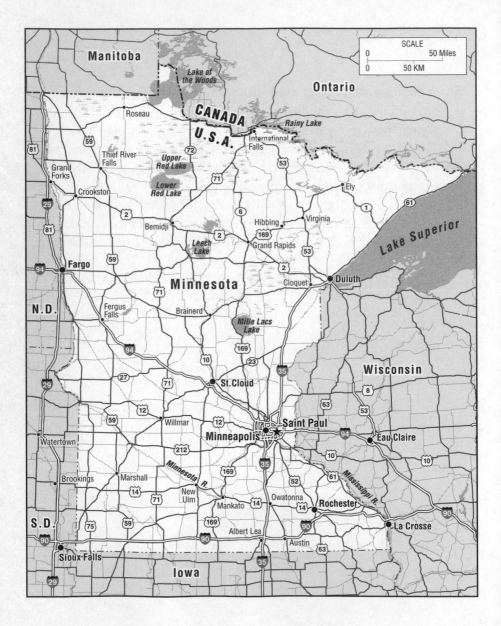

# Contents

*The St. Croix River from Interstate State Park.*

# Introduction

The name *Minnesota* comes from a Dakota word meaning "sky-tinted water." A very appropriate name for the land of 10,000 lakes—or 15,000 lakes, which would be more accurate. It's also a state of rushing rivers, with the Mississippi having its headwaters here, and the Minnesota and St. Croix Rivers flow through the Minnesota countryside as well. The terrain of the state varies wildly, from rolling, swooping roads and bluffs along the rivers to expansive prairies in the south and west to the dramatic hilly, forested vistas along the North Shore of Lake Superior, to the dense forests and wetlands of the northern part of the state. Most of the state's lakes and rivers were formed from glacial drift thousands of years ago, except for the southeast corner of the state, known as the Driftless Zone because of the absence of glacial drift.

The state's first inhabitants were the Anishinabe and Dakota tribes. Later the Ojibwa and Sioux made their way into the state, as did the European traders known as voyageurs. Tensions between the Europeans and the Native Americans make up an ugly part of the state's history, with the culmination in the Dakota War of 1862, which led to the largest mass execution in Minnesota and the deaths of hundreds more. The War is remembered and documented throughout south-central Minnesota.

Logging and farming were the two primary occupations in the early years, followed closely by mining in the northeastern part of the state and tourism around the Brainerd Lakes area. Industrialization increased in Minnesota after World War II, and resulted in more population growth in larger city centers. Some rural towns disappeared altogether, but others have found a way to, if not grow, at least remain stable and thrive.

This book takes you to many of those towns. These are villages and hamlets where you can find all manner of preserved history, in small historic museums and community centers. Although history is prevalent everywhere, a major reason to get outside the Twin Cities metropolitan area is, to put it mildly, to enjoy the view. Lakes and rivers; bogs and wetlands; dense old-growth forests; rolling hills full of trees and wildflowers; wide-open prairies—these are all to be found within the state's borders. The opportunities for outdoor recreation are nearly endless: hiking, biking, in-line skating, canoeing, swimming, fishing, hunting, camping, geocaching, backpacking, snowshoeing, sledding, skating, downhill and cross-country skiing, skijoring, dogsledding, snowmobiling, ice fishing—all year round, there's a way to enjoy the beauty Minnesota has to offer.

I truly loved researching this book. It was often exhausting, but it was never dull. Every corner I turned, I seemed to find something new and exciting. Until you've spent time "outstate" (which in Minnesota, means outside the Twin Cities metro area, you really haven't even begun to experience what Minnesota has to offer.

## Year-round Travels

As I said, you can travel the state year-round and find things to do. However, winter outstate can be a different beast than winter in the metro area. There's no disputing how beautiful it can be—miles of untouched snow, trees covered in hoarfrost, brilliant blue skies, and exhilaratingly intense sunsets over frozen lakes. But if you're planning on traveling outstate, especially to the western part of the state, keep a close watch on the weather: in areas where there are wide open spaces, particularly in the southwest, snowstorms can be windswept into zero visibility, and highways can sometimes be closed. Always travel with a winter safety kit in your car, which should include a fully charged cell phone, a flashlight and spare batteries, blankets (yes, multiple), a shovel, extra clothes in case you need to turn your car off, nonperishable snacks and bottled water, flares, rope, a knife of some sort, waterproof matches and candles, and a first-aid kit.

I don't mean to make traveling in winter in Minnesota sound like an especially dangerous or foolish thing to do. But use common sense—if the weather forecaster is sounding apocalyptic, it might be a good idea to try to travel earlier or postpone.

That said, summer is the peak time to visit many of these places, as travelers are drawn to warm, sunny days outdoors. In most areas, you'll find

*Rainy Lake.*

some of the visitor attractions (museums, restaurants) have limited or seasonal hours. When planning your trip in the winter months, be sure to confirm which sites are open and when, to avoid being disappointed.

One thing you can nearly always find open is a state park. Most of Minnesota's 70-plus state parks are open at least some of the time in the winter. And for good reason: winter recreation enthusiasts appreciate the opportunities to get out their cross-country skis or snowshoes and take in the natural beauty found in these parks. Many parks offer special winter activities and events, sometimes highlighting the area's history as viewed through a wintry lens.

## Finding Your Way

A good state map is essential, but if you really want to explore the back roads and byways, you're going to need more than that. Most of the county routes (designated throughout as CR) don't appear on state maps, because there's simply not enough room. One solution is, of course, GPS; however, that's not 100 percent reliable either. On my journeys, I was frustrated to be told I was on a road in another county altogether, and on one memorable trip, the GPS told me I wasn't on a road at all, although the view out the front windshield told me otherwise.

The best thing I did for these trips was to purchase county road maps from the Minnesota Department of Transportation (call 651-366-3017 for more information, or visit the website www.dot.state.mn.us/mapsales/). These were inexpensive and incredibly detailed, and got me out of being lost on many occasions. They are a bit bulky to carry around, but if you're wandering around a part of the state that has a bewildering number of county routes that don't show up on your state map, and your GPS has given up trying, these maps are invaluable.

*Fernberg Road, Ely.*

## Speaking of Roads . . .

The annual summer joke is that road construction is Minnesota's fifth season. Even though technology has improved to the point where some construction jobs can be done year-round, obviously summer is the prime time (if for no other reason than to fix the potholes created by winter turning into spring). Minnesota's Department of Transportation does an admirable job of updating their website (www.dot.state.mn.us) with roadwork around the state, and I'd strongly advise checking with them when planning specific routes and dates. There's nothing more dispiriting than coming on an unexpected, lengthy detour.

However, I wouldn't necessarily recommend trying to avoid detours, either; you never know what you might discover by going off the main route. It's just that it's more enjoyable if you know it's coming, and you're not scrambling to reach your bed & breakfast before the sun goes down on the very dark Gunflint Trail.

You'll find some roads are paved and in good condition. Others may be in need of work, and it makes sense to take things a bit more slowly. You'll also end up on some gravel roads, which are not necessarily the most comfortable drive, but worth it to get to your final destination.

## Routes and Timing

In each chapter, I've included an estimated length and distance. Take the word *estimated* very seriously. The length is of the "as the crow flies" variety, and the time assumes only a few stops with a moderate speed. If you want to visit most of the sites along each route, your time will increase, especially if you decide to enjoy some of the outdoor recreational opportunities. How much extra time? That's not for me to say— how long will you need to linger over artwork at the Minnesota Marine Art Museum in Winona, or spend climbing the Mount Rose Trail in Grand Portage, or browse the fun shops in Nisswa, or bike the Heartland Trail, or take a boat tour on Kabetogama Lake to see the Ellsworth Rock Gardens?

Finally, remember to be respectful of the places you visit. Signs in various state parks ask that you leave only footprints and take only pictures. If you're visiting a small historical museum, consider making a small donation to help them continue to operate and grow their collections. Thank your bed & breakfast proprietor and the staff at the local café who made you an amazing batch of pancakes with local maple syrup. These gems are all valuable, and we want them around for years to come.

*Hiking trail at Tettegouche State Park.*

CHAPTER 1

# The North Shore,
# Part 1: Hinckley to Lutsen

**Estimated length:** 95 miles
**Estimated time:** 2 hours

**Getting there:** From the Twin Cities, take I-35W north to Duluth, then follow old MN 61 north to Lutsen.

**Highlights:** The view overlooking Lake Superior; small shipping towns like Two Harbors; historic sites including Split Rock Lighthouse; and numerous points of natural beauty, including Gooseberry Falls and Palisade Head. This route can be extended by adding the Gunflint Trail, Grand Marais, and Grand Portage (see Chapter 2).

In a state that has lakes small and large, prairies, and rolling countryside, it's hard to pick one area as the most scenic. But the North Shore has arguably some of the loveliest vistas in the state, and the region is one of the state's most popular for visitors.

The eastern edge of the Arrowhead runs along the shores of Lake Superior. Much of the Lake Superior area was inhabited by the Ojibwa before the arrival of the Europeans, who came searching for trade routes and posts. The French were prominent explorers and settlers in this area, looking for furs and other goods for trade, and their influence is seen in community names like Grand Marais and Grand Portage. Fur trading was a central activity until about 1840, when most of the traders and trappers moved elsewhere, including the Mississippi headwaters area. However, the arrival of railroads in 1869, combined with increased ship traffic on Lake Superior, led to a population boom. The growth of commercial fishing as well as the development of the iron ore industry, combined with more sophisticated infrastructure and shipping methods, led not only to established communities but to the beginning of the tourism industry.

While fishing and mining enjoyed their heyday, the lumber and agricultural industries were booming as well, at least until the Depression years when competition in other parts of the country reduced their prominence.

Today's North Shore still sees considerable commercial fishing and mining activity. But tourism has come to play an ever-increasing role in the local economy. Whereas visitors used to come only in the summer for fishing and hiking, now they come year-round, taking advantage of the area's winter landscape for activities like skiing, snowmobiling, snowshoeing, and even dogsledding.

If you're traveling north from the Twin Cities via I-35W, it's worth a brief stop in **Hinckley** to visit the **Hinckley Fire Museum.** On September 1, 1894, a historic event occurred in this quiet logging town. A fire started, and while any fire that burns out of control in the wilderness can be considered a wildfire and therefore devastating, the fire that consumed Hinckley was worse. Its technical name is firestorm; flames shot up 4 miles into the air, and 20 square miles of land was destroyed in less than four hours. The firestorm evolved much like a natural disaster, with cyclones of fire advancing and wreaking havoc. The only other comparable firestorms in the 20th century were related to the launching of atomic bombs in Hiroshima.

The Hinckley Fire Museum is housed in a small building that previously served as the town's railroad depot (built to replace the one destroyed by the firestorm). Though small, it has a sizable collection of fire artifacts, as well as a brief documentary movie, and Native American items as well. The friendly staff knows the history of the firestorm well and is happy to answer questions or provide information on the individual artifacts.

Also worth a visit is **St. Croix State Park,** the largest of Minnesota's state parks at just over 34,000 acres. Hiking, biking, canoeing, horseback riding, and camping are all popular warm-weather activities, especially along trails that explore the **Kettle River** and **St. Croix River.** Winter finds the park attractive to cross-country skiers, snowshoeing enthusiasts, and snowmobilers.

You can also take a break from driving and visit the famed **Tobies,** conveniently located right on the interstate. Tobies today is a large operation, having grown from its location on a prominent tourist route. Its claim to fame is its cinnamon and caramel rolls, although self-nicknamed Halfway Stop now serves three meals a day, including breakfast 24 hours a day.

Hinckley is not a bad point to stop if you've left the Twin Cities late in the afternoon, especially if you planned ahead and reserved a room at either of two fine lodging choices. **Dakota Lodge** offers a wide variety of accommodations: four bed & breakfast lodge rooms, all with private bath and fireplaces; cabins; and a two-bedroom guesthouse. The bed & breakfast rooms come with a full breakfast daily. The property is a naturalist's haven, with easy access to nearby St. Croix State Park.

**Woodland Trails Bed & Breakfast** is a country charmer situated on 500 acres of woodland. The property includes 4 miles of trails for hiking as well as access to Grace Lake for bird-watching, paddleboating, or catch-and-release fishing. The five guest rooms all have private baths and electric fireplaces, and full breakfast is included.

Back on I-35W, enjoy the sweeping vista that greets you when you arrive in **Duluth:** the city sloping down to the harbor, the famous **Aerial Lift Bridge** that connects Duluth with neighboring Wisconsin, the sight of ore boats proceeding slowly through the canal, with sailboats large and small dotting the waters around them. Originally settled by Sioux and Ojibway tribe members, Duluth established itself as a central port for shipping in the United States in the mid-1800s. Besides being the only U.S. port to have access to both the Atlantic and the Pacific, Duluth was on the edge of large-scale lumber, grain, and mining operations that kept the city growing. In the early twentieth century, steel production further boosted Duluth's prominence. In the second half of the twentieth century, however, foreign competition in the steel industry had a severe impact on the city. Refocused efforts promoting the value of Duluth as a tourist destination, along with renovation of waterfront areas, brought new life to the area.

Duluth's shipping history is on display at the **SS *William A. Irvin*,** which spent more than 40 years delivering coal and iron ore as well as transporting dignitaries around the Great Lakes region. Today she's available for tours during the summer, and in October she becomes the "Ship of Ghouls."

Another facet of Duluth's history is available for exploration at the **Lake Superior Railroad Museum,** devoted to Duluth's locomotive history, including vintage wood-burning steam engines (including the largest one ever built), railroad snowplows, and an operating model train exhibit. Between Memorial Day and Labor Day, visitors can ride a vintage electric trolley around the museum, or sign up to take a ride on the North Shore Scenic Railroad, which has a number of options. Visitors who purchase a ride on the North Shore Scenic Railroad are eligible for discounts on museum admission.

A different aspect of Duluth's history can be found at **Glensheen.** Just north of downtown Duluth, on a stretch of Lake Superior shoreline, is the 39-room mansion Glensheen. Built in the early 1900s by the prosperous Congdon family, Glensheen is now open as a historical site. There are three levels of tours available: the house's exterior and grounds; the exterior, grounds, and first and second floors; or all of these plus the third floor, attic, and basement. The last tour takes the longest (and can be toasty in warmer weather—central air was not an available amenity when the mansion was built), but if you can manage it, it's worth the extra time. The docents are well trained and full of interesting tidbits about the history and construction of the 36-room mansion (as well as local history of the area), filled with mostly original furniture, decorating, and artwork. The grounds, set on a wide expanse of shoreline, include a rocky beach, a boathouse, a carriage house, and a gardener's home, as well as extensive, lavish gardens.

One thing that is not mentioned on the tour, but that you can now ask about at the end (in earlier years, docents were not allowed to talk about it), is the murder of Elisabeth Congdon and her nurse at Glensheen in 1977. For some, this is reason enough to visit Glensheen, but even if you have no interest in the real-life murder and subsequent trials, visiting Glensheen provides an unusually detailed and carefully preserved view of a lost way of life.

A great place to spend a sunny afternoon is **Canal Park.** This area, which surrounds the Minnesota side of the Aerial Lift Bridge, is full of small shops and restaurants, both for dine-in or to carry out and enjoy on a walk along the bridge's pier, or wandering down the **Lakewalk,** a 3-mile boardwalk that hugs the Lake Superior shoreline and runs the distance of downtown. Periodic stairways and paths provide access to additional shops and restaurants, and there are plenty of benches where you can rest and watch the boats going by.

Canal Park is also home to several shops that are browse-worthy. The **Dewitt-Seitz MarketPlace,** itself listed on the National Register of Historic Places, houses **Blue Heron Trading Co.,** a gift and cookware store; **North-**

## SIGHTS ALONG THE PARKWAY

**Skyline Parkway** is a short scenic byway that provides impressive views of Duluth and the harbor as it winds through residential and rural areas on the ridges above downtown Duluth. The parkway can be maddening to follow (it's not terribly well marked, although the city is working to remedy that), but it is worth the effort if you want to catch some spectacular views of Lake Superior, the city of Duluth, and western Wisconsin. Take a detailed Duluth map with you, and be aware that parts of the road are closed during the winter months. Along the way, you can visit **Enger Park,** a small but lush picnic area complete with its own stone tower (open for climbing, and the view is worth the effort). During the summer months, the floral display is breathtaking, and shaded picnic tables are spread generously throughout the grounds.

A large park set along Lake Superior, **Leif Ericson Park** has a wide variety of amenities: an open-air amphitheater that hosts live performances during the summer months, strolls along the lakeside, and a lovely and (in-season) fragrant rose garden.

ern **Waters Smokehaus,** a gourmet food shop; **J. Skylark Company,** a toy store, and **Art Dock,** featuring artworks and craft items by local artists. There are several good dining options. In Canal Park, you can stop by **Grandma's Saloon and Grill, Lake Avenue Café, Little Angie's Cantina,** or **Bellisio's.** Not far from the lakefront are **Fitger's Brewhouse and Grill** (part of a larger complex that includes shopping and lodging), **Pizza Luce, Burrito Union, Zeitgeist Arts Café,** and **Top of the Harbor,** a local institution at the **Radisson Hotel**—a restaurant at the top of the round hotel, which has a revolving venue for dining and aerial viewing. Not far from downtown is **At Sara's Table,** near the University of Minnesota campus and renowned for its work with locally sourced foods. Finally, just outside Duluth on Old MN 61 is the **New Scenic Café,** one of the area's best restaurants, so it's a good idea to make reservations.

Lodging is also plentiful, although plan ahead for weekends, even in winter. In Canal Park try the **Canal Park Lodge,** the **Inn on Lake Superior** (rooftop outdoor pool open year-round), or the **South Pier Inn.** On Duluth's east end, there are a number of turn-of-the-century bed & breakfasts (see sidebar, next page).

When it's time to move on from Duluth, find MN 61. While many

## BED & BREAKFASTS

In Duluth's east end is a stretch of historical houses (including the Congdon mansion, Glensheen). Within this area, not on Lake Superior itself but a short drive or doable walk, is a cluster of bed & breakfasts, most from the 19th or early 20th centuries and often built by the prominent citizens of the time.

**A. Charles Weiss Inn** was built by A. Charles Weiss, the former editor and publisher of the *Duluth Herald*. This inn, built in 1895, has five rooms with private bath. Massage is available by appointment.

The **Mathew S. Burrows 1890 Inn** has seen many changes since its days as a "bachelor pad," complete with third-floor ballroom, but it now offers five rooms, all with private bath.

The **Olcott House** includes luxurious accommodations in five suites in this home with private baths, as well as a separate carriage house suite. Several of the suites have fireplaces and whirlpool tubs; all have air conditioning, LCD TVs, and either four-poster or canopy beds.

The **Ellery House's** four elegant suites all have private baths, robes, and feather beds; one suite has a private sun porch, while another has a separate sitting area.

Built in 1909 by architect Edwin H. Hewitt, the **A. G. Thomson House** has four rooms with private bath in the main house as well as three rooms with private bath in the adjacent carriage house.

The **Cotton Mansion,** a 16,000-square-foot 1908 Italianate mansion, offers seven rooms and suites, all sumptuously appointed. A full breakfast is served each morning by candlelight, and an afternoon wine and cheese service is provided daily.

---

people think of this direction as heading north, it's actually northeast, and you might sometimes hear this route referred to as heading east. Note: there are actually two MN 61 routes. The official route runs parallel to old MN 61, but old MN 61 is a better choice, as it's closer to the shoreline of Lake Superior and gives a better view of the lakefront along the way. You'll see all manner of lakeshore lifestyle, from elaborate houses and resorts to decades-old fishing cabins and family-owned motels. There are several small towns in the early stretch of the drive, including **French River** and **Knife River,** towns built during the mining glory days and still alive today, thanks to fishing and tourism. In Knife River, stop at **Russ Kendall's**

**Smokehouse,** the oldest smokehouse on the North Shore and highly regarded, for some topnotch herring, smoked whitefish, or salmon.

A few miles north of Knife River is **Two Harbors,** an iron ore and fishing port. Staying on MN 61 doesn't take you to the scenic and historic heart of the town, so turn right on Waterfront Drive and continue a few blocks to the waterfront area, where you'll find a more typical waterfront small town. From Two Harbors, the view to the lake is focused on an enormous ore dock, still used today for taconite from the Iron Range. Dwarfed by the dock is the *Edna G.,* the last coal-fired, steam-powered tugboat, permanently anchored and available for tours seasonally. Nearby is the **Duluth and Iron Range Depot,** formerly the headquarters for that company, today home to the **Depot Museum,** a testament to the importance of railroads to the area.

From the Depot Museum, travel on South Avenue as it winds toward the shore until you reach the **Two Harbors Light Station.** First lit in 1892, the Light Station still lights up today, although automation has replaced the lighthouse keeper. The site today is a historic museum, open seasonally for visitors, and part of the lighthouse serves as the **Lighthouse Bed and Breakfast,** for guests who want to experience the history more closely.

The grounds and adjacent shoreline are worthy of exploration. A trail from the lighthouse leads you out to the rocky outcroppings, which are easy hiking (but use caution when the rocks are slippery), or you can take a walk along the water break into Lake Superior and get a better view of the shoreline and the iron ore dock.

Another unique lodging option is the **Northern Rail Traincar Bed and Breakfast,** which is exactly as described—a bed & breakfast built out of train cars. It is unusual for a B&B, in that it welcomes children. If

*Two Harbors Lighthouse Bed and Breakfast.*

you'd like more traditional lodging, the **Superior Shores Resort** has everything you need, including a prime location on the lakefront.

For meals, it's hard to beat the choices three times a day at the **Rustic
Inn Café,** and **Betty's Pies** has been famous for years for its pastries.

Returning to MN 61, a few miles northeast of Two Harbors you'll pass
through a massive tunnel carved into **Silver Cliff,** which, besides being an
impressive sight, also serves as the gateway to the "true" North Shore. The
drive will become more rolling, the scenery more dramatic as rock cliffs
tower over the narrow road, which passes over fast-flowing rivers and along
dense forests of ash, birch, aspen, and evergreens.

Shortly after you drive through Castle Danger (which, in spite of its
evocative name, doesn't appear to have a castle that causes danger), you'll
reach **Gooseberry Falls State Park.** This waterfall area is by no means the
largest waterfall in the United States, but it's visitor-friendly, with a sizable
visitors center and extensive trails and walkways. Pets are allowed, and there
are "doggie bags" strategically placed to encourage dog owners to clean up
after their pets. The park twists and turns around the base of the falls,
allowing access to both sides. Be sure to wear sturdy shoes; crossing wet
rocks is a tricky proposition in the best of footgear, and flip-flops could be
downright dangerous. Many visitors stay in the falls area, but if you have
the time, take the River View Trail to Agate Beach, where the Gooseberry
River flows into Lake Superior. The trail will take you high onto the cliffs
overlooking the river, then onto the beautiful stony beach.

Just a few miles north of Gooseberry Falls is another state park worth
visiting: **Split Rock Lighthouse State Park.** This small safety beacon for
passing ships is not large in stature, but situated on a dramatic, steep cliff, it
proved its worth for decades. Now it's open for tourists to visit, along with
a large visitors center with gift shop and video presentation. If you're feeling fit, take the trail that leads down the side of the cliff to the beach below
(171 steps each way) for amazing views of the lighthouse and the surrounding shorelines. The lighthouse grounds are connected to the Gitchi-
Gami State Trail, which can be used by bikers or inline skaters. The
lighthouse itself is rarely lighted anymore, but every year on the anniver-
sary of the sinking of the *Edmund Fitzgerald* (November 10), a ceremony
and lighting takes place.

As you drive northeast on MN 61, you'll arrive in Silver Bay. A stop at
the Chamber of Commerce (located on MN 61) will get you directions to
find the cemetery where John Beargrease is buried. Beargrease was a leg-

## HIKING ON THE NORTH SHORE

The North Shore is a hiker's (and biker's) paradise. There are trails looping up and down the shore, sometimes intersecting with one another, in and out of state parks and **Superior National Forest.** Many are short and meant for easy day hikes, but others offer more ambitious, longer-term plans. The **Superior Hiking Trail** is a collection of hiking byways and trails covering 277 miles along the Lake Superior shoreline from **Jay Cooke State Park** south of Duluth to the Canadian border west of Grand Portage. Frequent campsites and parking lots allow visitors to choose between backpacking and taking short day hikes, and there are loop trails that allow hikers to complete a circle in a short period of time. Contact the Superior Hiking Trail Association for information on its Lodge-to-Lodge Hiking Programs.

The **Gitchi-Gami State Trail** is a work in progress, with final plans to include 86 miles of nonmotorized trails extending from Two Harbors to Grand Marais. At press time, the Trail had various portions completed, some in unconnected chunks, the longest finished section located between Gooseberry Falls State Park and Beaver Bay, with a satellite trail leading to Split Rock Lighthouse State Park. Check the Gitchi-Gami Trail Association for updated information on completed sections and parking information.

endary mail carrier on the North Shore in the early 1900s, using sled dogs and, seasonally, canoes to bring the mail to the remote edges of the state. Duluth's famous John Beargrease Sled Dog Marathon, held each January, commemorates his accomplishments.

About 4 miles north of Silver Bay, look for signs on the right directing you to **Palisade Head.** Off MN 61, the road to Palisade Head is a short, narrow, gravel road that brings you to a parking lot and a scenic overlook off a 200-foot rock cliff formed by lava over a billion years ago. This is technically part of **Tettegouche State Park,** although it's not physically part of the park itself. This is a popular spot for rock climbers, but even if you don't climb, you'll be rewarded with the views near the parking lot at the top. On a good weather day, you can see Split Rock Lighthouse in the distance and the **Sawtooth Mountains** to the northeast, as well as Wisconsin's **Apostle Islands** directly east. If you're traveling with young children, hang on to them—Palisade Head does not have safety fences. For overnight arrangements, look no further than the **Baptism River Inn,** a beautiful log cabin bed & breakfast.

Tettegouche State Park is well worth a visit, aside from Palisade Head. The park has nearly every kind of natural feature—Lake Superior shoreline, waterfalls and rivers (including the 60-foot High Falls), mountainous hiking terrain, six inland lakes, and dense forests. There are 23 miles of hiking trails; in winter, cross-country skiers have access to 15 miles of trails. Snowmobilers and ATV users have limited trails to use as well.

Another lovely vista in the area is combined with a historic site. Near Schroeder you'll see a sign pointing the way to **Father Baraga's Cross**. Father Baraga was a Slovenian priest who took on the arduous task of ministering to a number of Ojibwa settlements in Minnesota, Wisconsin, and Michigan, often traveling by snowshoe or canoe. After surviving a devastating storm in his canoe when it was tossed by the wind into the mouth of the Cross River, Father Baraga erected a wooden cross in thanks, which

*Father Baraga's Cross.*

was later replaced with the granite cross that stands there today. A visit to the site in inclement weather could give you some idea what Father Baraga faced and why he was so thankful to have survived.

Not far from Father Baraga's Cross is **Temperance River State Park,** a heavily wooded park with trails for hiking, camping, snowmobiling, cross-country skiers, and rock climbers. To gain one of its best vantage points, take the trail that winds upstream from the parking lot until you reach the Temperance River gorge, incredibly narrow and leading to many spectacular waterfalls.

At first glance, **Lutsen** appears to be nothing more than a wide spot in the road, with a coffee shop and convenience store (where you can buy fish bait and yarn). But Lutsen is Minnesota's largest ski area, with 90 runs of varying difficulty across four mountains. Downhill skiers, snowboarders, and cross-country skiers have a thousand acres of land at their disposal, along with an Alpine Slide and a mountain tram for prime sightseeing. Lutsen isn't just popular in the winter, although that's its prime season; hiking, horseback riding, mountain biking, rock climbing, and kayaking and canoeing are all offered in the summer, when the lush greenery attracts skiers and nonskiers alike. What it lacks in "town" amenities, it more than makes up for in natural beauty and outdoor recreation. For lodging, there are many resorts that cater to skiers and hikers, including **Lutsen Resort, Solbakken Resort,** and **Caribou Highlands Lodge.** Nearly all the resorts in the area offer some kind of dining option, or you can cook your own if you've booked a condo or townhouse.

## IN THE AREA

### Accommodations

**A. Charles Weiss Inn,** 1615 East Superior Street, Duluth. Call 218-724-7016; 800-525-5243. Website: www.acweissinn.com.

**A.G. Thomson House,** 2617 East Third Street, Duluth. Call 218-724-3464; 877-807-8077. Website: www.thomsonhouse.biz.

**Baptism River Inn,** 6125 MN 1, Silver Bay. Call 218-353-0707; 877-353-0707. Website: www.baptismriverinn.com.

**Caribou Highlands Lodge,** 371 Ski Hill Road, Lutsen. Call 218-663-7241; 800-642-6036. Website: www.caribouhighlands.com.

**Cotton Mansion,** 2309 East First Street, Duluth. Call 218-724-6405; 800-228-1997. Website: www.cottonmansion.com.

**Dakota Lodge,** 40497 MN 48, Hinckley. Call 320-384-6052. Website: www.dakotalodge.com.

**The Ellery House,** 28 South 21st Avenue, Duluth. Call 218-724-7639; 800-355-3794. Website: www.elleryhouse.com.

**The Inn on Lake Superior,** 350 Canal Park Drive, Duluth. Call 218-726-1111; 888-668-4352. Website: www.theinnonlakesuperior.com.

**Lighthouse Bed & Breakfast,** 1 Lighthouse Point, Two Harbors. Call 218-834-4898; 888-832-5606. Website: www.lighthousebb.org.

**Lutsen Resort,** 5700 West MN 61, Lutsen. Call 218-663-7212; 800-258-8736. Website: www.lutsenresort.com.

**The Mathew S. Burrows 1890 Inn,** 1632 East First Street, Duluth. Call 218-724-4991; 800-789-1890. Website: www.1890inn.com.

**Northern Rail Traincar Bed and Breakfast,** 1730 County Route 3 (CR 3), Two Harbors. Call 218-834-0955; 877-834-0955. Website: www.northernrail.net.

**The Olcott House,** 2316 East First Street, Duluth. Call 218-728-1339; 800-715-1339. Website: www.olcotthouse.com.

**Solbakken Resort,** 4874 West MN 61, Lutsen. Call 218-663-7566; 800-435-3950. Website: www.solbakkenresort.com.

**South Pier Inn,** 701 Lake Avenue South, Duluth. Call 218-786-9007; 800-430-7437. Website: www.southpierinn.com.

**Superior Shores Resort & Conference Center,** 1521 Superior Shores Drive, Two Harbors. Call 218-834-5671; 800-242-1988. Website: www.superiorshores.com.

**Woodland Trails Bed & Breakfast,** 40361 Grace Lake Road, Hinckley. Call 320-655-3901. Website: www.woodlandtrails.net.

## Attractions and Recreation

**Gitchi-Gami State Trail.** Website: www.ggta.org.

**Glensheen,** 3300 London Road, Duluth. Call 218-724-8863. Website: www.d.umn.edu/glen/.

**Gooseberry Falls,** 3206 MN 61 East, Two Harbors. Call 218-834-3855. Website: www.dnr.state.mn.us/state_parks/gooseberry_falls/index.html.

**Hinckley Fire Museum,** 1060 Old Highway 61 South, Hinckley. Call 320-384-7338.

**Lutsen Mountains,** Ski Hill Road (CR 5), Lutsen. Call 218-663-7281. Website: www.lutsen.com.

**North Shore Commercial Fishing Museum,** 7136 MN 61, Tofte. Call 218-663-7804. Website: www.commercialfishingmuseum.org.

**S.S. William A. Irvin,** 301 Harbor Drive, Duluth. Call 218-727-0022. Website: www.williamairvin.com.

*The falls at Gooseberry Falls State Park.*

**Split Rock Lighthouse,** 3713 Split Rock Lighthouse Road, Two Harbors. Call 218-226-6372; 888-727-8386. Website: www.mnhs.org/places/sites/srl/index.htm.

**St. Croix State Park,** 30065 St. Croix Park Road, Hinckley. Call 320-384-6591. Website: www.dnr.state.mn.us/state_parks/st_croix/index.html.

**Stoney Creek Kennels,** 142 Sawbill Trail, Tofte. Call 218-663-0143. Website: www.stoneycreeksleddogs.com.

**Superior Hiking Trail.** Call 218-834-2700. Website: www.shta.org.

**Temperance River State Park.** MN 61, Schroeder. Call 218-663-7476. Website: www.dnr.state.mn.us/state_parks/temperance_river/index.html.

## Dining

**At Sara's Table,** 1902 East 8th Street, Duluth. Call 218-723-8569. American cuisine, locally sourced. Website: www.astccc.net.

**Bellisio's,** 405 Lake Avenue South, Duluth. Call 218-727-4921. Italian in a bistro setting. Website: www.grandmasrestaurants.com/bellisios.

**Betty's Pies,** 1633 MN 61, Two Harbors. Call 218-834-3367. Serving all three meals, but the pie is the main draw. Website: www.bettyspies.com.

**Bluefin Grille,** 7192 West MN 61, Tofte. Call 218-663-6200. American food with an emphasis on local, particularly Lake Superior seafood when available. Website: www.bluefinbay.com.

**Burrito Union,** 1332 East 4th Street, Duluth. Call 218-728-4414. Mexican food, including breakfast. Website: www.burritounion.com.

**Fitger's Brewhouse and Grill,** 600 East Superior Street, Duluth. Call 218-279-2739. Open daily for lunch and dinner. Hearty sandwiches, burgers, and quesadillas all available with your choice of brew. Website: www.brewhouse.net.

**Grandma's Saloon & Grill,** 522 Lake Avenue South, Duluth. Call 218-727-4192. American cuisine. Website: www.grandmasrestaurants.com.

**Lake Avenue Café,** 394 Lake Avenue South, Duluth. Call 218-722-2355. Upscale American. Website: http://lakeavenuecafe.com.

**Little Angie's Cantina,** 11 East Buchanan Street, Duluth. Call 218-727-6117. Website: www.grandmasrestaurants.com/littleangies.

**New Scenic Café,** 5461 North Shore Scenic Drive, Duluth. Call 218-525-6274. Contemporary American. Website: www.sceniccafe.com.

**Pizza Luce,** 11 East Superior Street, Duluth. Call 218-727-7400. Excellent pizza, including gluten-free and vegan options. Website: www.pizzaluce .com.

**Tobies,** 404 Fire Monument Road, Hinckley. Call 320-384-6174. Website: www.tobies.com.

**Top of the Harbor,** 505 West Superior Street (in the Radisson Hotel), Duluth. Call 218-727-8981. American cuisine.

**Zeitgeist Art Café,** 222 East Superior Street, Duluth. Call 218-722-9100. Part of a larger arts building, serving gourmet American food. Website: www.zeitgeistartscafe.com.

## Other Contacts

**Gitchi-Gami Trail Association,** Silver Bay. Website: www.ggta.org.

**Hinckley Convention and Visitors Bureau,** P.O. Box 197, Hinckley. Call 320-384-0126. Website: www.hinckleymn.com.

**Lutsen Tofte Tourism Association,** 7136 West MN 61, Tofte. Call 888-616-6784. Website: www.americasnorthcoast.org.

**Superior Hiking Trail,** Two Harbors. Call 218-834-2700. Website: www.shta.org.

**Two Harbors Chamber of Commerce,** 1331 MN 61, Two Harbors. Call 218-834-6200. Website: www.twoharborschamber.com.

**Visit Duluth,** 21 West Superior Street, Duluth. Call 800-438-5884. Website: www.visitduluth.com.

Devil's Kettle Waterfall at Judge Magney State Park.

CHAPTER

2

# The North Shore, Part 2: Grand Marais, Grand Portage, and the Gunflint Trail

**Estimated length:** 95 miles
**Estimated time:** 2 hours

**Getting there:** From the Twin Cities, take I-35W north to Duluth. From Duluth, take MN 61 along the North Shore to Grand Marais and Grand Portage. From Grand Marais, take County Route 12 (CR 12, also known as the Gunflint Trail) to Trail's End.

**Highlights:** The lakeshore town of Grand Marais, with its shops, art galleries, and excellent restaurants; the Devil's Kettle Waterfall at Judge C.R. Magney State Park; Grand Portage National Monument and the view of the monument from the Mount Rose Trail; a leisurely drive along the Gunflint Trail with a stop at the Chik-Wauk Museum and Nature Center. (Note: if you have ample time, you could combine this route with the Hinckley to Lutsen route in Chapter 1.) Enjoy the sights while listening to the local radio station, WTIP, which does an excellent job of covering local events and history in rotation with an eclectic selection of music.

Note: If you're planning on venturing into the Boundary Waters, it's strongly recommended that you purchase the Superior National Forest Visitor Map. Published by the USDA in conjunction with Superior National Forest, it is an incredibly detailed map of the Boundary Waters Canoe Area

Wilderness (BWCAW). (It wouldn't hurt to buy a magnifying glass to use with it.) The BWCAW is full of trails and portages, rivers and streams, that don't appear on most state maps and can get you lost unless you're very familiar with the area. Many local gas stations and convenience stores sell it, as do BWCAW permit offices, or contact the Superior National Forest headquarters in Duluth (218-626-4300) for information on ordering one.

The terrain on the approach to **Grand Marais** on MN 61 is some of the most beautiful and dramatic in the state. The road offers periodic pull-offs with scenic overlooks, and there's much to see: rivers flowing into Lake Superior, massive stone bluffs with towering pine trees and hard-woods, and the Sawtooth Mountains in the distance. Fishing, fur trading, lumber, and mining have all played a part in the development of the area, but despite that, there are miles and miles of untouched wilderness in the Arrowhead portion of the state. The remnants of the state's ancient geological history are in full display here: the magnificent stony cliffs were formed millions of years ago due to volcanic activity. The volcanoes are long gone, but the cliffs are holding firm. Summer in this part of the state is generally more temperate than anywhere else, and it's not uncommon to find lodgings that don't have air-conditioning, simply because it isn't necessary. The flip side to that pleasant scenario is that winter can be very cold, with heavy snowfall. But that doesn't deter outdoor enthusiasts from exploring the Arrowhead in winter; there are stores in Grand Marais that can properly and safely outfit you for the cold, and the region is full of cross-country skiing, snowshoeing, and snowmobiling opportunities.

It can be surprising for the first-time visitor to arrive in Grand Marais and find it to be far more civilized than they might have expected, given its remote location. But Grand Marais has a reputation not just as a great jumping-off point for outdoor recreation, but as an arts community. There are many artists who live here year-round, and more that arrive in the warmer months. The support of the arts has extended to a wider definition of art, including culinary and folk art skills. These factors, combined with the easy-living harbor location, make Grand Marais a favorite in the state.

**North House Folk School** is a nonprofit organization working to rekindle interest and develop skills in old-style crafts and survival techniques. Over 200 courses are offered each year, some as short as a day, some taking several days. Courses include not only how to cook and bake in an outdoor brick oven, but how to build the oven; constructing kayaks and canoes; building yurts and a facsimile of Thoreau's cabin; knitting, paper-

*Sailboat in the fog at the Grand Marais harbor.*

making, jewelry, and ancient Native American techniques for basket weaving. Students come from all over the United States to learn these ancient skills and enjoy the harborside lifestyle.

More traditional art studies can be found at the **Grand Marais Art Colony.** Like North House, the Grand Marais Art Colony offers classes year-round in visual arts, book arts, ceramics, glass, and printmaking. Classes are available for children and adults.

The **Grand Marais Playhouse** is a 40-year-old theater group that offers performances just about every month of the year, with a range of drama to comedy to musicals. The Playhouse also offers summer theater workshops.

One of the most scenic overlooks in the town is **Artists' Point,** a short walk along the harbor to the Coast Guard parking lot, where a trail takes you .5 mile over lava rock and through a forest with breathtaking views of the harbor and the coastline. Its name came from the number of artists—visual, literary, and musical—who come here again and again for inspiration.

Art galleries are plentiful too. The **Betsy Bowen Studio and Gallery,** the **Blue Moose,** the **Sivertson Gallery, Eight Broadway Gallery,** and **Boreal Light Imagery Gallery** are just some of the galleries showcasing local (as well as regional and some national) artists. These galleries are just steps from one another in the easily walkable downtown of Grand Marais. Note: many galleries are closed in the early winter months—check ahead if you're planning a winter visit.

Other stores can help you with the more practical aspects of your stay. Part souvenir shop, part outfitter for wilderness experiences, the **Lake Superior Trading Post** is staffed with friendly people who know their stock. The log cabin construction gives it a north woods feel, and Lake Superior is right outside the door. The **Gunflint Mercantile** is a food store for backpackers and general visitors alike. Come in for the free fudge sample, view the extensive supply of lightweight foods for the trail, and stay for the coffee and soup. **Wilderness Waters** is one-stop shopping for outdoor survival gear, from books and maps to clothing and gear. The store also provides canoe outfitting services.

There are plenty of casual choices in Grand Marais too. **My Sister's Place** isn't much to look at on the outside, but it has friendly service and

---

### FINE DINING IN GRAND MARAIS: LOCAL, SUSTAINABLE, ORGANIC

The food scene in Grand Marais is impressive, especially given its size and location. Talented chefs are increasingly exploring the more remote outposts in the northeast, and they're bringing creativity and a willingness to work with locally sourced foods for their inventive menus. The **Angry Trout Café** has indoor or outdoor dining, with a strong focus on local ingredients and sustainability. And be sure to check out the artsy bathrooms. **Chez Jude** is small in size, but big in flavor. Proprietor Judi Barsness brings an international flair to her locally inspired menu. Afternoon tea provides the option of a traditional British tea or a North Shore tea complete with smoked trout and lingonberry jam. A well-chosen wine list and good selection of microbrews completes the experience. The **Dockside Fish Market & Deli** is a retail market that also has a deli with a limited but delicious menu, including several varieties of fish caught in Lake Superior. The **Gunflint Tavern** is a friendly, casual restaurant with an innovative menu using organic foods when possible. The **Crooked Spoon** offers contemporary American cuisine, presented as dress-up food in a casual atmosphere.

---

solid soups and sandwiches that will satisfy any taste and appetite (including some vegetarian options, such as the "Fungi" mushroom sandwich). The specialty of the house is burgers, and there are 24 variations to choose from. **Sven and Ole's** is the quintessential Grand Marais experience. Contrary to the name, this is no bland Scandinavian fare, but a local pizza haunt with hearty, flavorful pizzas with Scandinavian names: *uffda Zah,* anyone? The menu does include an option for a lutefisk pizza, but unless you have the $1 million in cash, better to order one of the other offerings. Entrées start at $5. The **Wild Onion Café** in the Harbor Inn serves hearty breakfasts, salads, soups, sandwiches, and entrées include variations on old favorites, such as the Salmon BLT and the Sol Burger, made with venison and deep-fried pickles. It also offers outdoor dining, a great option for this harborside spot.

Finally, your sweet tooth will be sated with a trip to the **Pie Place.** This pie shop gives Betty's Pies in Two Harbors serious competition. Flaky crusts, traditional and innovative fillings will leave you wanting more. Or you can venture into **World's Best Donuts.** No matter that the name doesn't seem modest; the doughnuts are truly wonderful. The walk-up window opens at 4:30 AM.

Lodging choices vary from traditional hotels and motels to condos to bed & breakfasts. Right on the harbor is **East Bay Suites,** all of which have decks or patios overlooking the lake as well as full kitchens, fireplaces, washers and dryers, and WiFi. Accommodations vary in size from studio to three bedrooms, with some suites offering bunk beds. Nearby is **Cobblestone Cove Villas,** a newer townhouse property with upscale accommodations in easy walking distance to the shops and restaurants of Grand Marais.

**Opel's Lakeside Cabins** are just north of Grand Marais on Croftville Road. Opel's has five cabins available, all directly on the Lake Superior shoreline. The cabins are rustic but charming, and the views and location are hard to beat.

Bed & breakfasts are available too. In Grand Marais itself is **Bally's B & B,** built in 1912 and offering four rooms with private bath. **MacArthur House B & B** has five rooms with private bath, and a common-area fireplace and Jacuzzi. **Skara Brae** is a small but charming Scottish-themed bed & breakfast east of Grand Marais on MN 61 that offers, for adults and children ages 12 and up, lovely accommodations in two rooms and a cottage, all with private bath. Breakfast and afternoon tea are available daily,

## NANIBOUJOU LODGE

Even in an area with eclectic lodging options (see, for example, the yurt on the Gunflint Trail), **Naniboujou Lodge** stands apart both for its physical building and for its history. It's listed on the National Register of Historic Places, and its colorful past matches its bright interior. Built in the 1920s as a private club for founding members that included Babe Ruth and Jack Dempsey, the club never reached its potential as the country reached the Depression years. Eventually reborn as a hotel and lodge, Naniboujou has a beautifully decorated Great Hall, painted in designs reflective of Cree Indian culture, with vivid primary and jewel colors, and it also has the state's largest native rock fireplace. The rooms are tastefully and comfortably set up, and there are no TVs or telephones in order to preserve the sense of getting away from it all. The dining room, open in the summer, serves hearty home-cooked food. Although it's close to a state park with excellent hiking trails, you might

*The great room at Naniboujou Lodge.*

find yourself tempted to just relax on the extensive, peaceful lawns, soaking in the Lake Superior views from your Adirondack chair.

and discounts for North House Folk School students are offered. A bit farther east is the **Superior Overlook B & B,** just 200 feet from the Lake Superior shore, offering two rooms with private baths and a common area with sauna and sun deck.

East and north of Grand Marais are an abundance of state parks and wildlife areas. Be sure to check local conditions before visiting—nearly annual droughts have brought severe fire restrictions in parks and campsites in recent years, and some park access is limited during wildfires. Check with individual parks for up-to-the-minute information.

Depart Grand Marais on MN 61 heading east to find **Judge C.R. Magney State Park**, located between Grand Marais and Grand Portage and home to the **Brule River.** The Brule leads to **Devil's Kettle,** a unique 50-foot waterfall that is rumored to have a bottomless cauldron. Nine miles of hiking trails, including an ascent to Devil's Kettle, are open during season, as well as several fishing sites. Campsites are available; advance reservations are recommended.

The naturalists on hand during the summer months at **Grand Portage State Park,** the only Minnesota state park managed jointly with a Native American tribe, are tribe members that can speak about local Ojibwa history. The northern boundary of the park is the **Pigeon River,** which is also the international boundary with Canada. The park's 120-foot High Falls can be viewed by hiking the Falls Trail, which has a 700-foot boardwalk as the final section and three overlooks. Camping is not available, but the falls are easily accessible for day visitors via .5-mile trail and boardwalk.

Not far from the monument is **Grand Portage Lodge & Casino.** Located just south of the Canadian border, the Grand Portage Lodge has spacious rooms and a friendly staff ready to help with anything you need. The hotel offers an indoor pool and sauna, a full-service restaurant overlooking Lake Superior, and a seasonal (mid-May to mid-October) RV park. The casino takes the north woods theme and runs with it, including a northern lights display in the carefully designed ceiling. Open 24/7, the casino offers a shuttle to Thunder Bay, Ontario (U.S. citizens will need passports to cross the border).

If you're looking for lodging that's a bit quieter, reserve a room at the **Hollow Rock Resort,** just a few miles south of the Casino. Hollow Rock has five cottages, all with lake views and some with decks on the lake.

Returning to Grand Marais, it's time to travel inland from the lake and explore the route known as the **Gunflint Trail.** A 57-mile paved road leading from Grand Marais to Saganaga Lake near the Canadian border, the Gunflint Trail is hands down one of the most beautiful drives in the region. With acres of forest uninterrupted by only the occasional café or shop, the Trail also has an extensive collection of lodging options nestled within the trees. Watch your speed as you drive; it's not unusual to have a deer, wolf, or even a moose appear on the road, and all of these animals can do as much harm to you and your vehicle as you can do to them. The area has enjoyed a growth in year-round tourism, thanks to the increased popularity of winter sports, which have joined the ranks of favored pastimes

## GRAND PORTAGE NATIONAL MONUMENT

*Grand Portage National Monument as seen from the Mount Rose Trail.*

Continuing east on MN 61 will bring you to the **Grand Portage National Monument,** one of only two national monuments in the state (the other, Pipestone National Monument, is in the exact opposite southwest end of the state; see Chapter 16). This monument is really a don't-miss for visitors to the area. An extensive re-creation of the life of traders and Native Americans before there was a United States and Canada, the National Monument has a traditional Ojibwa village, a reconstruction of the Northwest Company's stockade (including a great hall and kitchen), a fur trade canoe under construction, and historic gardens that represent what the original trading villages grew. Kids' programs are offered in the summer, and costumed historical guides are available to answer questions. Trails outside the stockade take visitors deep into the northern wilderness, and there are snowshoe trails available during the winter. The National Monument also serves as the departure point for the ferry to Isle Royale, which is the largest island in Lake Superior (and technically is part of Michigan). One of the best views of the monument is provided by attraction hiking trail across the street from the entrance: the **Mount Rose Trail.** This short (.5 mile) but very steep trail leads hikers to an overlook at the top that provides stunning views of the monument, the Sawtooth Mountains, and Lake Superior. Keep an eye out as you drive along the water for areas of wild rice growing.

such as birding, mountain biking, fall foliage viewing, canoeing and kayaking, camping, fishing, and even mushroom and berry picking.

It's also the gateway to the eastern edge of the **Boundary Waters Canoe Area Wilderness.** The Boundary Waters is an amazing natural preserve, encompassing over a million acres of woods (all contained within the Superior National Forest) and at least 2,500 of Minnesota's famed lakes, teeming with wildlife. It is largely meant to be explored traveling as the explorers of old did: by canoe, with backpack and tent. While a few areas have opened up to motorized vehicles, the beauty of this area is the peacefulness allowed by the absence of motors, letting visitors hear the myriad bird calls and wolf howls, and the sound of water and wind.

It is possible to day-trip in the Boundary Waters, or least along the edges, by starting from Ely or the Gunflint Trail (see Chapter 3 for the former). More ambitious travelers may want to portage in with canoes and set up camp. Experienced canoers and campers can plot their routes, but if you're fairly new to this type of adventure, you might consider working with an outfitter, who can also reserve a permit for you. Permits for camping visitors are required in order to limit the number of entrances into the BWCAW each day, in an effort to keep the wilderness, well, wild. See the sidebar for details.

---

## BWCAW OUTFITTING

Visitors to the Boundary Waters, except for day-only visitors, need to reserve a permit ahead of time. You can contact the Boundary Waters Canoe Area Wilderness Permit Reservation Center (877-550-6777; www.bwcaw.org), or you can work with one of the following Gunflint Trail outfitters to make arrangements.

**Boundary Country Trekking** is run by Ted and Barbara Young, proprietors of the Poplar Creek Guesthouse. They offer a variety of adventure arrangements in the Gunflint Trail/Boundary Waters area and can organize lodge-to-lodge hiking and biking trips, canoe/biking trips, mountain biking, and canoeing trips.

**Clearwater Canoe Outfitters & Lodge** offers both a lodge and an outfitting company. The proprietors can assist you with canoeing, hiking, fishing, birding, even wildlife photograph trips.

**Seagull Outfitters** is owned by Debbie Mark, who grew up in the business and has extensive personal experience throughout the BWCAW. Her location at the far end of the Gunflint Trail provides some deep wilderness exploration opportunities.

---

You can drive for miles down the Gunflint Trail and see few, if any, other cars or people. It might look like miles and miles of forest and wilderness, but if you plan ahead, there are plenty of recreational stops to make. There are several hiking options available, including the local portion of the **Superior Hiking Trail,** the longest hiking trail in the Midwest at over 200 miles. But there are many other hiking trails to choose from, some of which overlap or intersect the Superior Trail. Stop at any of the lodges along the Trail (or check with the visitor center in Grand Marais) to pick up a Gunflint Trail hiking map that details each route, how long and how difficult it is, and what you're likely to find there.

Fifty-five miles down the 57-mile trail, you'll reach CR 81. Turn right, and you'll shortly be at the entrance to the **Chik-Wauk Museum and Nature Center.** Housed in a lodge built in 1934, Chik-Wauk opened in its new capacity in 2010. It's small but packed with displays about the history of the Gunflint Trail, including artifacts, interactive and hands-on exhibits, and video and written histories of local pioneers. The grounds of Chik-Wauk surround a bay of Saganaka Lake and offer five short hiking trails of varying difficulty (including one ADA trail).

At the very end of the trail is **Trail's End Café.** The knotty pine interior fits well with the wooded wonderland outside, and the Trail's End serves basic but hearty meals, including burgers, sandwiches, and pizzas.

Camping is certainly an option, but if you'd prefer a building over a tent, there are many options hidden away along the trail, including bed & breakfasts. **Poplar Creek Guest House** is tucked into a peaceful wooded area and has two guest rooms, each with private bath and a suite. The rooms are graciously appointed, and they share a common room with kitchenette, fireplace, and private deck. The suite has a private kitchen

## HAM LAKE BURN

Toward the western end of the trail, you'll drive through the remnants of the 2007 **Ham Lake Burn.** The fire was set accidentally, but its devastation was thorough. The area was suffering from a drought, and the rapidly spreading fire burned through more than 36,000 acres on the U.S. side (75,000 acres in total), the largest fire in nearly a century. A fire of this magnitude requires time for recovery, and you will see the stark outlines of burned tree shards, as well as the hopeful signs of green growth beginning to appear on the ground beneath them.

area as well as a deck. The proprietors also have a cabin for rent, as well as the **Tall Pines Yurt.** For a true wilderness experience, the Tall Pines Yurt is open year-round for summer or winter adventures. Four guests can sleep on bunk beds or a futon, although additional bedding can be provided for more guests. A fully equipped kitchen is included; an outhouse is steps away, as is a traditional Finnish sauna. **Pincushion Bed & Breakfast** is on 43 acres just 3 miles from Grand Marais and, sitting on the Sawtooth Mountain ridgeline, has impressive views and on-site access to hiking trails. This peaceful inn has four rooms, all with private bath, and a common living area with fireplace. **Cross River Lodge** is situated on Gunflint Lake. This property offers two lovely bed & breakfast rooms, each with private bath, and four cabins near or on the lake with fireplaces, complete kitchens, and decks with barbecues.

*Hiking Trail at the Chik-Wauk Museum and Nature Center.*

Lodges are common accommodations along the trail, usually offering both hotel rooms and cabin lodging. These lodges tend to be full service, providing not only a place to sleep, but restaurants, outfitting services, guide services, and equipment rental. **Old Northwoods Lodge** has bed & breakfast rooms in its lodge and housekeeping cabins, as well as a full-service restaurant. **Bearskin Lodge** is a model of peace and retreat. The resort has 11 cabins and two lodges with town house accommodations. There's a hot tub and sauna on-site, and massage can be arranged. During the summer, boats, canoes, and pontoons are available, as well as bikes; children's naturalist programs can be arranged. **Gunflint Lodge** has 23 cabins with varying amenities, from the more rustic Canoers Cabins (bunk beds, shared bath in a nearby building) to the Romantic Cottages (lake-view cabins with fireplace, hot tub, and full kitchen), to the Gunflint Lake Home (with two

*Bearskin Lodge on the Gunflint Trail.*

to four bedrooms, fireplace, hot tub, and sauna). A restaurant on-site offers an alternative to self-cooking in the cabin, and an extensive list of year-round activities includes winter and summer sports as well as massage. A beautiful stone patio adjacent to the bar is the perfect end-of-day stop.

## IN THE AREA

### Accommodations

**Bally's B & B,** 121 East 3rd Street, Grand Marais. Call 218-387-1817.

**Bearskin Lodge,** 124 East Bearskin Road, Gunflint Trail. Call 218-388-2292; 800-338-4170. Website: www .bearskin.com.

**Clearwater Canoe Outfitters & Lodge,** 774 Clearwater Road, Gunflint Trail. Call 218-388-2254; 800-527-0554. Website: www.canoebwca.com.

**Cobblestone Cove Villas,** 17 South Broadway, Grand Marais. Call 218-387-2633; 800-247-6020. Website: www.cobblestonecovevillas.com.

**Cross River Lodge,** 196 North Gunflint Lake Road, Gunflint Trail. Call 888-238-5975. Website: www.crossriverlodge.com.

**East Bay Suites,** 21 Wisconsin Street, Grand Marais. Call 218-387-2800; 800-414-2807. Website: www.eastbaysuites.com.

**Gunflint Lodge,** 143 South Gunflint Lake, Gunflint Trail. Call 218-388-2294; 800-328-3325. Website: www.gunflint.com.

**Hollow Rock Resort,** 7422 East MN 61, Grand Portage. Call 218-475-2272. Website: www.hollowrock.biz.

**MacArthur House B & B,** 520 West 2nd Street, Grand Marais. Call 218-387-1840; 800-792-1840.

**Naniboujou Lodge,** 20 Naniboujou Trail, Grand Marais. Call 218-387-2688; www.naniboujou.com.

**Old Northwoods Lodge,** 7969 Old Northwoods Loop, Gunflint Trail. Call 218-388-9464; 800-682-8264. Website: www.oldnorthwoods.com.

**Pincushion Bed & Breakfast,** 968 Gunflint Trail. Call 218-387-1276; 800-542-1226. Website: www.pincushionbb.com.

**Poplar Creek Guest House,** 11 Poplar Creek Drive, Gunflint Trail. Call 800-322-8327. Website: www.littleollielodging.com.

**Skara Brae,** 1708 East MN 61, Grand Marais. Call 218-387-2861; 866-467-5272. Website: www.skarabraebb.com. This small but charming Scottish-themed bed and breakfast offers, for adults and children ages 12 and up, lovely accommodations in two rooms and a cottage, all with private bath. Breakfast and afternoon tea are available daily, and discounts for North House Folk School students are offered. Rates start at $75.

**Superior Overlook B & B,** 1620 East MN 61, Grand Marais, Call 218-387-9339; 877-387-9339.

**Tall Pines Yurt,** 11 Poplar Creek Drive, Gunflint Trail. Call 800-322-8327. Website: www.littleollielodging.com.

## Attractions and Recreation

**Chik-Wauk Museum and Nature Center,** 28 Moose Pond Drive, Grand Marais. Call 218-388-9915. Website: www.chikwauk.com.

**Grand Marais Art Colony,** 120 3rd Avenue West, Grand Marais. Call 218-387-2737. Website: www.grandmaraisartcolony.org.

**Grand Marais Playhouse,** 51 West 5th Street, Grand Marais. Call 218-387-1284. Website: www.arrowheadcenterforthearts.org/playhouse/.

**Grand Portage Casino,** Grand Portage. Call 800-543-1384. Website: www.grandportage.com.

**Grand Portage National Monument,** 211 Mile Creek Road, Grand Portage. Call 218-387-2788. Website: www.nps.gov/grpo.

**Grand Portage State Park,** 9393 East MN 61, Grand Portage. Call 218-475-2360. Website: www.dnr.state.mn.us/state_parks/grand_portage/index.html.

**Judge C.R. Magney State Park,** 4051 East MN 61, Grand Marais. Call 218-387-3039. Website: www.dnr.state.mn.us/state_parks/judge_cr_magney/index.html.

**North House Folk School,** MN 61, Grand Marais. Call 218-387-9762; 888-387-9762. Website: www.northhouse.org.

## Dining

**Angry Trout Café,** 416 West MN 61, Grand Marais. Call 218-387-1265. Website: www.angrytroutcafe.com.

**Chez Jude,** 411 West MN 61, Grand Marais. Call 218-387-9113. Internationally inspired, locally sourced. Website: www.chezjude.com.

**The Crooked Spoon,** 17 West Wisconsin Street, Grand Marais. Call 218-387-2779. Contemporary American cuisine. Website: www.crooked spooncafe.com.

**Dockside Fish Market & Deli,** 418 West MN 61, Grand Marais. Call 218-387-2906. Retail market and deli focused on local fish. Website: www .docksidefishmarket.com.

**Gunflint Tavern,** 111 Wisconsin Street, Grand Marais. Call 218-387-1563. Website: www.gunflinttavern.com.

**Sven and Ole's,** 9 West Wisconsin Street, Grand Marais. Call 218-387-1713. Local pizza institution. Website: www.svenandoles.com.

**Trail's End Café,** 12582 Gunflint Trail. Call 218-388-2212; 800-346-6625. Basic but hearty meals, including burgers, sandwiches, and pizzas. Website: www.wayofthewilderness.com/cafe.htm.

**The Wild Onion Café,** 207 Wisconsin Street, Grand Marais. Call 218-387-1191. Hearty cafe food. Website: www.bytheharbor.com/rest.html.

**World's Best Donuts,** 10 East Wisconsin Street, Grand Marais. Call 218-387-1345. Website: www.worldsbestdonutsmn.com.

## Other Contacts

**Boundary Country Trekking,** 11 Poplar Creek Drive, Grand Marais. Call 218-388-4487; 800-322-8327. Website: www.boundarycountry.com.

**Boundary Waters Canoe Area.** Website: www.canoecountry.com.

**Clearwater Canoe Outfitters & Lodge,** 774 Clearwater Road, Grand Marais. Call 218-388-2254; 800-527-0554. Website: www.canoebwca.com.

**Grand Marais Area Tourism Association.** 13 North Broadway Avenue, Grand Marais. Call 888-922-5000. Website: www.grandmarais.com.

**Gunflint Trail Association,** 13 North Broadway Avenue, Grand Marais. Call 800-338-6932. Website: www.gunflint-trail.com.

**Seagull Outfitters,** 12208 Gunflint Trail, Grand Marais. Call 218-388-2216; 800-346-2205. Website: www.seagulloutfitters.com.

The view from Lake Vermilion State Park.

CHAPTER

3

# Western Boundary Waters: Highway 1 to Ely

**Estimated length:** 80 miles
**Estimated time:** 3 hours

**Getting there:** South of Grand Marais, near Illgen City, take MN 1 northwest to Ely. From Ely, take MN 169 south to MN 135, then to County Route 21 (CR 21) to Embarrass.

**Highlights:** The densely wooded area along MN 1, the Dorothy Molter Museum, International Wolf Center, and the North American Bear Center; the Soudan Underground Mine State Park; and the cold spot of the nation, Embarrass.

South of Grand Marais, MN 61 connects with MN 1, a stretch of highway that veers inland from Lake Superior to Ely, a gateway city into the Boundary Waters. Note: Please see the note on the Superior National Forest Visitor Map at the beginning of Chapter 2 if you are planning to visit the Boundary Waters Canoe Area Wilderness for advice on a critically important map of the Wilderness.

When driving along MN 1 (also known as the Ely-Finland Trail), it's hard to imagine there was ever a time when this area was decimated by logging; today, the forests are thick along the road, with pine, spruce, birch, and aspen trees that tower over the narrow highway. (Note: in some places, the trees are very close to the road, thus providing excellent camouflage for deer, so take your time.) But it only increases in intensity as you near Ely and the edge of the Boundary Waters.

The route to Ely takes you through **Superior National Forest.** This massive forest, more than 3 million acres, could just as easily have been named the Forest of Lakes—there are more than two thousand lakes and countless connecting streams and rivers in this area, routes used for water travel thousands of years ago. Voyageurs used these waterways as their trade routes back and forth to Canada, and loggers used them to transport logs to mills. The forest itself is on the southern edge of the boreal forest biome, which also extends across northern Asia and Europe. It contains a complex mix of vegetation that veers from stands of mostly hardwood trees to mostly conifers, varying according to the soil composition.

*The forests on MN 1.*

Within the forest, wildlife thrives. More than 350 species of birds, reptiles, mammals, and amphibians have been identified, along with 50 species of fish; with luck, you can spot a gray wolf or moose, great gray owls or boreal chickadees. The lakes are full of walleye and trout and even lake sturgeon.

After just a few miles on MN 1, you'll arrive at the little town of **Finland.** Not surprisingly, this town was founded by Finnish settlers. It's home to one of Minnesota's more tongue-in-cheek annual festivals, **St. Urho's Day.** The festival is Finland's response to Ireland's St. Patrick's Day and celebrates a fictional saint who reportedly drove the grasshoppers out of Finland (the country). Finland (the town) has a statue of this mythical saint and every March celebrates his accomplishments.

From Finland, turn onto CR 7 and drive 7 miles to visit **George Crosby Manitou State Park.** The land was donated by mining executive George

Crosby, and from the time of its designation as a state park, it was treated differently from other state parks. The decision was made to design it as a park specifically for backpackers and limit overall development. Consequently, there is no central campground, but instead a collection of primitive campsites scattered throughout, accessible only by foot. There are 24 miles of hiking trails, including 5 miles of the **Superior Hiking Trail,** that run through rugged terrain, through old-growth forests, and along the Manitou River and Benson Lake.

Returning to MN 1 and continuing north, you'll cross the **Laurentian Divide,** which marks the dividing line between waters that flow north to Hudson Bay and those that flow south to Lake Superior. A few miles farther, watch on the left for the sign directing you to Forest Road 106, a gravel road that takes you to **McDougal Lake,** a beautiful undeveloped lake with a mile-long hiking trail exploring the forest along the shoreline.

As you draw closer to Ely, you'll cross the **South Kawishiwi River,** which is a lovely sight itself. The South Kawishiwi River Campground has campsites that can be reserved and some that are held for drop-in visitors. The campground marks an entry point into the **Boundary Waters Canoe Area Wilderness** to the north. For more information about good reference materials and permits, please see the Boundary Waters information at the beginning of Chapter 2.

At one time the city of **Ely** was primarily a logging and mining town. Today, tourism is a major force because of its proximity to the BWCAW. But even if your goal is to get to the wilderness, allowing some time to spend in Ely is a good idea. There's plenty to see and do.

If you're planning on heading into the BWCAW, there are several local outfitters that can help with equipment, permits, and guiding if needed. **Piragis Northwoods Company** is a large outfitting shop sells and/or rents all manner of outdoor gear, including canoes and camping gear. Piragis also offers guided canoeing and camping trips in the BWCAW. **Kawishiwi Lodge and Outfitters** is located on an entry point to a nonmotorized lake and can handle complete or partial outfitting. **Canadian Waters** can get you to any of the Boundary Waters entry points and handles complete and partial outfitting as well as fly-in canoe trips. **Boundary Waters Guide Service** specializes in fully outfitted guided tours. **Jordan's Canoe Outfitters** will work with any size group and any level of outfitting and guiding need.

Canoeing, camping, and fishing are popular activities, but the area is also full of excellent hiking trails, everything from short, gentle hikes to overnight hikes through rugged terrain. Cross-country skiing opportunities replace hiking in the winter. One particularly scenic hike is the **Kawishiwi Falls Hiking Trail,** east of Ely on CR 18 (also known as Fernberg Road). The trail is short, barely a mile, but travels to the edges of Fall Lake and Garden Lake, where steep cliffs overlook Kawishiwi Falls and the nearby power plant. Another interesting vantage point is found on the **Secret/Blackstone Hiking Trail,** further east on CR 18 and turning left onto Moose Lake Road. Here you can hike trails that will give you a glimpse of how the forest is gradually changing after the 1999 Blowdown, when storms blew down millions of trees across nearly 40 percent of the BWCAW. In some areas, every single mature tree was downed. However, where the blown trees are decaying, new life is growing.

*Kawishiwi Falls.*

In Ely, there's a unique piece of Boundary Waters history at the **Dorothy Molter Museum.** This is a loving tribute to the last person who lived in the Boundary Waters. Dorothy Molter lived a great deal of her adult life in a cabin in the BWCAW, and even though the U.S. government evicted other tenants when the area was declared a wilderness, she was granted lifetime tenancy. During her many years in her rustic cabin, she brewed homemade root beer for boaters and fishers coming through her area, earning the nickname "the root beer lady." After her death, her log cabin was painstakingly disassembled and reassembled on the eastern edge of Ely and turned into a museum. The cabin is crammed full of Dorothy's things, and the adjacent gift shop sells books about her as well as cases of root beer (worth the purchase). The only downside is the noise of traffic from nearby MN 169, which can make visitors (this one, at least) wonder why they couldn't have sited the museum just a bit farther down the road in an effort to recapture something more like the peace enjoyed by Molter in this natural setting.

Ely has two internationally acclaimed wildlife centers. The **International Wolf Center** is focused on wolf education and information. The center tries to address public fears and concerns about wolf behaviors through media relations and public visits. There are hands-on exhibits and "wolf cams" in the center's beautiful building, allowing visitors to watch wolves from a great distance; they also coordinate Learning Vacations, which bring visitors into the wilderness to meet "ambassador" wolves.

Similar in intent to the International Wolf Center is the **North American Bear Center,** one mile west of Ely. The Bear Center was founded by Dr. Lynn Rogers, a bear expert who has studied bears in and around Ely for many years. Although the building itself isn't as lavish as the Wolf Center, the Bear Center offers extensive and lively videos and exhibits including a look at the troubling case of Alaska's Grizzly Man. Staff and researchers are passionate and do an excellent job of making learning about bears fun. The "bear cams," streaming live on the center's website, have brought international attention to the Center in recent years, especially when black bear Lily gave birth live on the Internet. Be sure to watch the bears in their two-acre habitat from the viewing deck.

From Ely, travel south on MN 169 to visit the **Soudan Underground Mine.** The Soudan Mine gives visitors insight into the daily life of miners in this once operational mine. Adventurous tourists can take the tour, which carries them 27 stories beneath the ground (note: extensive walking

*Ted, one of the residents of the North American Bear Center.*

is required, including through confined areas). Those who don't wish to go below can wander the grounds for free. The scenery from the hillside mine is breathtaking, particularly during fall foliage season. The mine is part of the **Soudan Underground State Park,** which is adjacent to (and will eventually be part of) Minnesota's newest park, **Lake Vermilion State Park.** Once this park is fully open, the two parks will have almost 10 shoreline miles on beautiful Lake Vermilion.

For a different kind of animal adventure, make winter plans at the **Wintergreen Dogsled Lodge.** With nearly 30 years of dogsled adventures under their belt, the proprietors of the Wintergreen Dogsled Lodge know a thing or two about taking visitors on a dogsled trip, whether it's first-timers or seasoned sledders. Trips can be arranged with stays at the lodge itself, just east of Ely, as lodge-to-lodge treks, or as camping excursions. Multiple-night or one-day-only trips available, and theme trips (parent–daughter, photography) can be arranged as well.

Not surprisingly, the Boundary Waters area is surrounded by countless places to stay, everything from rustic mom-and-pop resorts to more elaborate deluxe accommodations.

Just outside the city of Ely is **Grand Ely Lodge,** the largest in Ely with 61 rooms and suites. The resort is very family friendly, with kids under 10 staying and eating free with paid adults. There's an indoor pool and sauna, and lake activities are provided at the marina on Shagawa Lake. The Evergreen Restaurant is open all day; there's also a lounge. Mountain bikes are available to guests who want to use the Trezona Trail across the street, which connects to the International Wolf Center.

Right in the heart of downtown Ely, the **Adventure Inn** is a small but charming property spread across two buildings, one a log-cabin-style building with north woods themes, and the newer space a solar building with Scandinavian themes. Not far away is **A Stay Inn Ely,** designed around the concept of a hostel, but with private rooms and baths. Each room has a color theme, and the Indigo Room would be appreciated by anyone who loves cozy attic spaces. The inn has a large gathering room and full kitchen for guests, as well as a spacious deck.

A few miles outside Ely, there are several beautiful and diverse lodging choices. The **Timber Trail Lodge** has 15 cabins ranging from one to six bedrooms as well as four motel units with kitchenettes. The resort can arrange boat rentals and guides; massage is offered on-site, and once-weekly float plane rides are offered to guests. The **Blue Heron Bed & Breakfast** has five beautifully decorated rooms, some with exposed log walls. Rooms come with private baths, lake views, full breakfast, use of canoes or snowshoes, and use of the sauna.

For those truly wanting the wilderness experience, **Log Cabin Hideaways** provides hand-hewn log cabins on the edge of the BWCAW. Each cabin comes with a canoe, but no electricity or indoor plumbing. Propane is provided for cooking; most units have a Finnish sauna. Some of the cabins are accessible by water only. But none of the cabins have neighbors; each cabin is on its own secluded site.

Seemingly in the middle of nowhere, **Fortune Bay Resort and Casino** is on Lake Vermilion and offers attractive rooms and suites, an indoor pool, dining room, 24-hour casino, and golf course. An on-site marina has fishing boats, pontoons, canoes, and paddleboats available for rent, or you can bring your own boat and dock it at the marina.

Ely has several dining choices in town. The **Chocolate Moose** is a

## BURNTSIDE LODGE

West of Ely, on Burntside Lake, **Burntside Lodge** has been offering gracious hospitality to guests since 1911, and it's arguably one of Minnesota's most famous accommodations. It's also family owned and has been since 1941. It has always been known as a relatively elegant resort, and in its early days was host primarily to professionals like doctors and lawyers. Today the resort offers several cabins in varying sizes, all tucked into the woods or near the lake; the peaceful ambience is enhanced by the lack of TVs or telephones. The lodge is on the National Register of Historic Places, due to its long history as a full-service resort, and also because the log buildings were built by local builders, using local materials, and have been impeccably maintained. The dining room (open daily for dinner in-season, weekends only for breakfast) serves delicious food in a large, open room. The adjoining gift shop has several items of local interest.

popular cabin-like restaurant serving casual lunch and dinner daily in hearty portions during the summer. Look for the vegetarian enchiladas—and consider sharing them or taking leftovers back to your cabin. **Sir G's** serves Italian food, including pasta made on-site. Ely has its own brewpub too: the **Boathouse Brewpub,** brewing its own beers and serving up good pub food. One of the cozier spots in Ely is **Front Porch Coffee and Tea,** an inviting coffeehouse with a limited but tasty menu of soups and pastries. If steakhouse fare is what you want, the **Ely Steak House** fits the bill with fresh fish specials, prime rib on weekends, and steak whenever you like. One of the newer options is **Rockwood,** which has a high-tech means of ordering: servers carry handheld devices which transmit orders immediately to the kitchen.

Ely has several blocks of shops, with a good variety of merchandise, from regular tourist things like shirts and mugs to specialty items, like art and model train supplies. The **Brandenburg Gallery** showcases the award-winning nature photography of Jim Brandenburg, who has traveled the world for *National Geographic* and who has a special love for the Boundary Waters area (he makes it his home part of the year). **Wintergreen Designs** produces its high-quality and attractive outdoor apparel in Ely and sells it at this local retail store (another store is open in Duluth). **Lisa's Second-Floor Bookstore** is on the second floor of Piragis. This bookstore is accessible only by going through the outfitting store. A small but congenial gathering space for book lovers, the shop has a solid selection of both fiction and local resource books. **Steger Mukluks & Moccasins** sells footwear inspired by Native American designs. Made in Ely from moose hide, its shoes are highly regarded for their comfort and winter protection.

## IN THE AREA

### Accommodations

**A Stay Inn Ely,** 112 West Sheridan Street, Ely. Call 888-360-6010. Website: www.stayinnely.com.

**Adventure Inn,** 1145 East Sheridan Street, Ely. Call 218-365-3140. Website: www.adventureinn-ely.com.

*The gathering room at A Stay Inn Ely.*

**Blue Heron Bed & Breakfast,** 827 Kawishiwi Trail, Ely. Call 218-365-4720. Website: www.blueheronbnb.com.

**Burntside Lodge,** 2755 Burntside Lodge Road, Ely. Call 218-365-3894. Website: www.burntside.com.

**Fortune Bay Resort Casino,** 1430 Bois Forte Road, Tower. Call 800-555-1714. Website: www.fortunebay.com.

**Grand Ely Lodge,** 400 North Pioneer Road, Ely. Call 218-365-6565; 800-365-5070. Website: www.grandelylodge.com.

**Log Cabin Hideaways,** 1321 North CR 21, Ely. Call 218-365-6045. Website: www.logcabinhideaways.com.

**Timber Trail Lodge,** 629 Kawishiwi Trail, Ely. Call 218-365-4879; 800-777-7348. Website: www.timbertrail.com.

### Attractions and Recreation

**Dorothy Molter Museum,** MN 169, Ely. Call 218-365-4451. Website: www.rootbeerlady.com.

**The International Wolf Center,** 1396 MN 169, Ely. Call 218-365-4695. Website: www.wolf.org.

**North American Bear Center,** 1926 MN 169, Ely. Call 218-365-7879. Website: www.bear.org.

**Soudan Underground Mine,** MN 169, Soudan. Call 218-753-2245. Website: www.dnr.state.mn.us/state_parks/soudan_underground_mine/index.html.

**Wintergreen Dogsled Lodge,** 1101 Ring Rock Road, Ely. Call 218-365-6022; 800-584-9425. Website: www.dogsledding.com.

## Dining

**Boathouse Brewpub,** 47 East Sheridan Street, Ely. Call 218-365-3894. Website: www.boathousebrewpub.com.

**The Chocolate Moose,** 101 North Central Avenue, Ely. Call 218-365-6343. Open summer only daily for all three meals. A popular cabin-like restaurant serving casual lunch and dinner daily during the summer.

**Ely Steak House,** 216 East Sheridan Street, Ely. Call 218-365-7412. Steakhouse and bar with fresh fish specials, prime rib on weekends, and steak whenever you like. Website: www.elysteakhouse.com.

**Front Porch Coffee and Tea,** 343 East Sheridan Street, Ely. Call 218-365-2326. Website: www.frontporchcoffeeandtea.com.

**Rockwood,** 302 East Sheridan Street, Ely. Call 218-365-7772.

**Sir G's,** 520 East Sheridan Street, Ely. Call 218-365-3688. Italian food, including pasta made on-site.

## Other Contacts

**Boundary Waters Canoe Area.** Website: www.canoecountry.com.

**Boundary Waters Guide Service,** Ely. Call 218-343-7951. Website: www.boundarywatersguideservice.com.

**Canadian Waters,** 111 East Sheridan Street, Ely. Call 218-365-3202; 800-255-2922. Website: www.canadianwaters.com.

**Ely Chamber of Commerce,** 1600 East Sheridan Street, Ely. Call 800-777-7281. Website: www.ely.org

**Jordan's Canoe Outfitters,** 1701 MN 1, Ely. Call 218-365-6677; 800-644-9955. Website: www.jordansoutfitters.com.

**Kawishiwi Lodge and Outfitters,** 3187 Fernberg Road, Ely. Call 218-365-5487. Website: www.lakeonecanoes.com.

**Piragis Northwoods Company,** 105 North Central Avenue, Ely. Call 218-365-6745; 800-223-6565. Website: www.piragis.com.

**Superior National Forest,** 8901 Grand Avenue Place, Duluth. Call 218-626-4322. Website: www.fs.fed.us.

*Kayaks on sale at Piragis.*

*Lake Kabetogama.*

CHAPTER

4

# International Falls and Voyageurs National Park

**Estimated length:** 80 miles
**Estimated time:** 3 hours

**Getting There:** From the Twin Cities, take I-94 west to exit 178 and head northeast on MN 24 until you reach US 10. Follow US 10 to Little Falls, then follow MN 371 north to US 2 west. In Bemidji, turn onto US 71 north to International Falls. From International Falls, take MN 11 east until the road ends for the southwestern tip of Rainy Lake; returning to International Falls, travel south on US 53 to County Route 122 (CR 122) north to reach Kabetogama.

**Highlights:** The border town of International Falls, with the Bronko Nagurski Museum and tours of the Boise Cascade Paper Mills; Rainy Lake; Voyageurs National Park; and Kabetogama Lake.

If you're coming from the Twin Cities, you have quite a drive to get to this part of the state, but it's well worth it. The land east of International Falls is stunning, with roller-coaster hills winding along the **Rainy River** and then reaching **Rainy Lake** itself. Historically it was a valued route, especially by the voyageurs after whom the national park was named. It was also an important area for lumber mills, with the convergence of both miles of trees and the power of the Rainy River. The Boise Cascade Paper Mill has been a decades-long employer in the community, still benefiting from that location. Missionaries were in abundance centuries ago too, looking to convert Native American tribes, and immigrant farmers sought out fertile land.

Does it get cold in the winter? Well, yes. Although there are trademark dustups with a town in Colorado, International Falls has been referring to itself as the Icebox of the Nation for years, although they get some competition in the coldest community contest with the town of Embarrass, to the southeast. But even the cold can be good for business; several auto manufacturers routinely test their vehicles in the winter here to make sure they can function in extreme weather.

The residents of this region have learned to adapt, and outdoor recreation is plentiful in the cold months. This is a part of the state where you can ski, snowmobile, and, most importantly, ice fish, which is made more comfortable by renting heated ice houses.

**International Falls,** named for a waterfall that used to be visible on the Rainy River but is now submerged in a reservoir, is right on the Canadian border and is a customs stop. Travel between the two countries is heavy; in fact, the International Falls international rail port is the second busiest in the entire country. The two countries have a good-natured relationship that in recent years has culminated in an annual **International Tug of War** contest, in which a 1,500-foot rope is strung across Rainy River with about 50 people on each side trying to pull the other side into the river.

The community's history is on display at two side-by-side museums: the **Koochiching County Historical Museum** and the **Bronko Nagurski Museum**. These two museums share one building, each focused on history specific to the region. Bronko Nagurski is a local legend, a farm boy who became one of the best professional football players in the sport's history. His side of the museum details not only his life and sports career, but the impact of the times (the Depression, World War II) on his life and that of others. The County Historical Museum has a well-rounded collection of artifacts reflecting the area's history with Native Americans and French voyageurs, as well as its relationship to Canada. Museum volunteers and staff are well versed in the collections and can answer questions and offer insightful tales.

**Boise Cascade,** one of the world's largest paper-making companies, offers both mill tours and woodland tours. Call ahead for reservations— these tours are very popular.

Not surprisingly, this area is full of activities in the great outdoors, some more rustic than others. If golf is your game, stop by **Falls Country Club.** Designed by Joel Goldstrand, the Falls Country Club golf course is a challenging and beautiful course, and it's open to the public. The course is filled with pine trees, and streams wind throughout.

You can stay in International Falls, but the lodging choices are mostly limited to chains like Holiday Inn, Days Inn, and Super 8. Most accommodations that provide more of the "northern" experience are on the outskirts, or along Highway 11 east to Voyageurs National Park.

Traveling out of International Falls on MN 11, enjoy the eastern portion of the **Waters of the Dancing Sky Scenic Byway.** This byway, which stretches most of the way across the Minnesota side of the border, narrows and curves its way along the Rainy River and Rainy Lake, with the road becoming hillier as you approach the eastern end.

There are good options for meals. **Giovanni's** is a cheerful, family-friendly, American-Italian restaurant with pizza, pasta, pierogies, and burgers. A buffet is available, as is an arcade area for kids. The **Coffee Landing** is a full-service coffee, espresso, and tea shop, along with a limited but tasty food menu including breakfast items, pastries, and quiche. The **Rose Garden Restaurant** serves classic Chinese American food, large portions at reasonable prices. The **Chocolate Moose Restaurant Company** sells platter-sized portions of pancakes, burgers, pasta, and dinner entrées, including steak and shrimp.

A few miles outside International Falls is the small town of **Ranier,** which sits near where Rainy River flows out of Rainy Lake. Taking a quick visit to this quiet little town, it's hard to believe it once was a destination for Prohibition-era bootleggers smuggling whiskey from Canada. The bridge used by the bootleggers is now the oldest cantilevered bridge in the world. Befitting a bootlegging community, Ranier used to be quite the wild town, full of saloons and bordellos. Today it's more of a haven for artists, with amenities geared toward the outdoor enthusiast. You can stay at **Woody's Rainy Lake Resort,** which has seven cabins with full kitchens, all near or on Rainy Lake. The lodge has a pub with pizza and beer, and is the headquarters for Woody's Fairly Reliable Guide Service. The tongue-in-cheek name reflects the jovial nature of Woody's resort, but is an understatement in terms of service; Woody's knows Rainy Lake, and they can help with summer and winter fishing needs. Across the street is the **Rainy Lake Inn & Suites at Tara's Wharf,** which offers four suite accommodations in a

*Downtown Ranier.*

charming "seaside" setting. The ice cream shop will keep everyone happy. **Grandma's Pantry** is open for most meals, but its specialty is enormous breakfasts.

For a heartier dinner, stop by **Almost Lindy's** on Crystal Beach, east of Ranier, a BBQ and pizza joint.

The last stretch of MN 11 is dotted with small resorts, private cabins, and year-round homes. There are several excellent lodging choices here, all with river and lake access and plenty of outdoor amenities. **Camp Idlewood** has nine cabins with knotty pine interiors and full kitchens; the resort itself has a beach, canoe, paddleboat, and inner tubes and tow ropes available at no fee. Boats and motors can be rented, or you can bring your own; each cabin has one dock space included, and additional spaces can be rented. **Bear Ridge Guest House** offers just two accommodation choices but is nevertheless a great choice for visitors to Rainy Lake. Located on a hill overlooking the lake, with a private deck to enjoy the view, Bear Ridge has a guesthouse suite with separate bedroom, full kitchen, and fireplace; a separate guest room has its own bath and living area. Actually located 12 miles east of International Falls, **Island View Lodge and Cabins** sits on the edge of Rainy Lake with gorgeous views and direct lake access. There are 15 cabins available, as well as several lodge rooms. An adjacent spa has a hot tub and sauna, and the lodge has a dining room and lounge. Literally where MN 11 ends is **Sha Sha Resort,** which has the unique advantage of being surrounded by water on three sides. Log cabins are graciously appointed, and there is a very private cabin a mile north of the resort itself. Sha Sha also has an extensive multi-tiered deck overlooking Rainy Lake, complete with deck bar and boat-in docks. The restaurant knows exactly how to cook walleye.

Rainy Lake also provides access to Minnesota's only national park,

## THE HOUSEBOAT LIFESTYLE

To really relax and enjoy the waters of Rainy River and Rainy Lake, consider booking a houseboat. Rainy Lake has two companies that have several houseboats available for rental. **Northernaire Houseboats** offers 10 houseboats of varying sizes and levels of amenities that hold anywhere from two to 12 people, including some with open decks and some with screened-in decks. Rentals include a tow-behind boat, free delivery on the lake twice weekly (for groceries and so on), and a guide service for the first 4 miles to orient you to the maps and buoy systems. Order ahead, and your boat's kitchen will be stocked with foods and beverages of your choice.

**Rainy Lake Houseboats** has several fully equipped houseboats that are more yacht-style and have kitchens, a tow-behind boat, swim platforms and waterslides, and deck table and chairs. Houseboats are available for two to 12 guests; some rent by the day, others with a three-day minimum or by the week. Guide service is available with prearrangement, and groceries can be ordered ahead as well.

**Voyageurs National Park.** Some of the oldest exposed rock formations in the world can be found here, carved out by the departures of at least four glaciers, leaving behind a series of four connected lakes. Centuries ago, French traders paddled these waters on their way to Canada, looking to trade animal pelts and goods with the natives. Today Voyageurs National Park is a haven for those who love to be on the water, whether by canoe, kayak, or houseboat. Hikers, snowshoers, and cross-country skiers travel the grounds year-round. A series of connected lakes and bays, as well as miles of untouched forest, provide an intimate north woods experience. Wildlife is abundant.

There are three visitors centers. Located 10 miles east of International Falls, the **Rainy Lake Visitor Center** is the primary source and the only one open year-round. The **Kabetogama Lake Visitor Center,** on the southwest shores of **Kabetogama Lake,** and the **Ash River Visitor Center,** on the **Ash River,** are both open late May through September only.

From the Rainy Lake Visitor Center, you can take the **Oberholtzer Trail,** named after a northern Minnesota conservationist. The trail winds through the forest and alongside marshes, with views of the Black Bay Narrows. Other available trails can be reached only by boat, including **Black**

Bay Beaver Pond Trail, which guides hikers to an active beaver pond; Anderson Bay Trail, which climbs a steep cliff with the reward being amazing views of Rainy Lake; and Little American Island, which explores the historic site of the Little American Gold Mine.

Another option for seeing the natural beauty of the park is to reserve a spot on one of the three tour boats offered during the summer season. You can also pick up last-minute tickets at either the Rainy Lake or Kabetogama Lake Visitor Centers, but any departures from the Ash River Visitor Center must be booked ahead of time.

Campgrounds are available on a first-come, first-served basis (groups can reserve ahead of time with one of the visitors centers), but note that the campgrounds within the park are only accessible by boat. A free permit is required for camping, which can be obtained at the visitors centers or at self-permit stations within the park. If you're interested in camping but would rather be able to drive up to your campsite, look into reserving a site at the Woodenfrog State Campground on CR 122. Located in Kabetogama State Forest, part of Voyageurs National Park, Woodenfrog has campsites available from mid-May to mid-September that don't require boat access. If you stop by the Woodfrog campgrounds, be sure to visit the Woodenfrog Refectory, a beautiful stone concession area built during the Depression by the Civilian Conservation Corps.

You can explore the northern part of the park via the Rainy Lake entrance, or you can return to International Falls and head south on US 53 to CR 122 and visit the southwest parts of the park, around beautiful

## ELLSWORTH ROCK GARDENS

From the southern end of Kabetogama, you can take a boat to the north shore of the lake and visit **Ellsworth Rock Gardens,** built over 20 years by Jack Ellsworth, who designed and constructed more than 60 terraced flower beds on a stony outcrop, filling them with more than 13,000 flowers and surrounding them with 200 abstract rock sculptures. After Ellsworth's death in 1974, the gardens languished; the national park service bought the property in 1978 and moved the buildings away, but it wasn't until public pressure mounted that the reclamation effort began in 1996. Since 2000, the park service has had an annual "Garden Blitz" day, where contractors and volunteers converge on the Gardens to keep them from reverting to forestland.

*The Woodenfrog Refectory at Kabetogama Lake Campgrounds.*

**Kabetogama Lake.** Birders should seek out the **Echo Bay Trail** near the Kabetogama Lake Visitor Center, which is an especially good area for sighting birds, as there's a great blue heron rookery along the way. A longer (nearly 28 miles altogether) and more difficult hike, the **Kab-Ash Trail** connects the Kabetogama and Ash River areas and gives hikers generous access to the park. Many trails are open not just for hiking in the summer, but cross-country skiing and snowshoeing in the winter.

Lodging is abundant around Kabetogama Lake, with many mom-and-pop resorts and cabins available for rent. **Voyageur Park Lodge** has ten cottages along Lake Kabetogama that, along with a lodge suite, offer guests peaceful privacy. Full kitchen, barbecue grills, and campfire sites are included with each cabin (campfires only when conditions allow). Use of canoes, kayaks, and paddleboats is free; fishing boats, pontoons, and motors can be rented on-site. **Herseth's Tomahawk Resort** offers eight cabins and one mobile home. The resort has a large sand beach with free canoes and paddleboats, and motorized boats are available for rent. The proprietor is a certified scuba diver and is happy to arrange diving excursions into Lake Kabetogama.

**Moosehorn Resort** has nine cabins stretched along Lake Kabetogama with a sandy beach. This is an especially family-friendly resort, located in a quiet bay that keeps the lake waters calmer than in other spots. Canoes, kid-sized kayaks, and a playground area are included for guests. Boats are available for rental. **Kec's Kove Resort** has eight cabins and a lodge with whirlpool and sauna. A massage therapist is available for guests, and motorized boats are available for rent. If you go fishing and need some help afterwards, Kec's can provide fish cleaning and freezing services. Paddle-boats, canoes, and kayaks are complimentary. **Northern Lights Resort, Outfitting, and Youth Quest** has ten cabins along Lake Kabetogama and a number of planned activities for all interest levels: guides can be arranged for fishing or other expeditions; a Ladies' Pontoon Cruise is offered weekly, with coffee and muffins; an adults' social cruise is also offered weekly in the evening; and the Youth Quest program is offered for kids ages 5 to 17, with planned events including kayaking, canoeing, tomahawk-throwing training, and island cookouts. Younger kids are separated from the older kids, and activities are age appropriate.

## IN THE AREA

### Accommodations

**Americinn,** 1500 US 71, International Falls. Call 218-283-8000; 800-331-4443. Website: www.hiifalls.com.

**Bear Ridge Guest House,** 210 Fourth Avenue, International Falls. Call 218-286-5710. Rates start at $110. Website: www.bearridgeguesthouse .com.

**Camp Idlewood,** 3033 CR 20, International Falls. Call 218-286-5551. Website: www.campidlewood.com.

**Herseth's Tomahawk Resort,** 10078 Gappa Road, Ray. Call 218-875-2352; 888-834-7899. Website: www.hersethstomahawkresort.com/.

**Island View Lodge and Cabins,** 1817 MN 11 East, International Falls. Call 218-286-3511; 800-777-7856. Website: www.rainy-lake.com.

**Kec's Kove Resort,** 10428 Gamma Road, Kabetogama. Call 218-875-2841; 800-777-8405. Website: www.kecscove.com.

**Kettle Falls Hotel,** 10502 Gamma Road, Voyageurs National Park. Call 218-240-1724. Website: www.kettlefallshotel.com.

**Moosehorn Resort,** 10434 Waltz Road, Kabetogama. Call 218-875-3491; 800-777-7968. Website: www.moosehornresort.com.

**Northern Lights Resort, Outfitting, and Youth Quest,** 12723 Northern Lights Road, Kabetogama. Call 612-805-9646; 800 318-7023. Website: www.nlro.com.

**Northernaire Houseboats,** 2690 CR 94, International Falls. Call 800-854-7958. Website: www.northernairehouseboats.com.

**Rainy Lake Houseboats,** 2031 Town Road 488, International Falls. Call 218-286-5391; 800-554-9188. Website: www.rainylakehouseboats.com.

*Northernaire Houseboats.*

## KETTLE FALLS HOTEL

The most unique lodging option is the **Kettle Falls Hotel.** Accessible only by boat or plane and located on an odd geographical twist that allows you to stand on the Minnesota side and look south to Canada, this hotel is the only lodging within Voyageurs National Park. It's located near the Kettle Falls and dams, which were built about the same time as the hotel. Nearly a century old, Kettle Falls Hotel has a rich history, starting with its construction in 1913 by timberman Ed Rose and, it's rumored, financed by the infamous Nellie Bly. Rose in turn sold the hotel to Robert Williams for $1,000 and four barrels of whiskey, which set the stage for the years to come, with bootleggers selling whiskey during Prohibition. Today it's on the National Register of Historic Places. The hotel has 12 rooms with shared baths, a full-service restaurant, and a saloon that still bears the marks of wilder early years.

**Rainy Lake Inn & Suites at Tara's Wharf,** 2065 Spruce Street Landing, Ranier. Call 218-286-5699; 877-724-6955.

**Sha Sha Resort,** 1664 MN 11 East, International Falls. Call 218-286-3241; 800-685-2776. Website: www.shashaonrainylake.com.

**Voyageur Park Lodge,** 10436 Waltz Road, Kabetogama. Call 218-875-2131; 800-331-5694. Website: www.voyageurparklodge.com.

**Woody's Rainy Lake Resort,** 3481 Main Street, Ranier. Call (218-286-5001; 866-410-5001. Website: http://fairlyreliable.com.

## Attractions and Recreation

**Boise Cascade Paper Mill,** Second Street, International Falls. Call 218-285-5011.

**Koochiching County Historical Museum/Bronko Nagurski Museum,** 214 Sixth Avenue, International Falls. Call 218-283-4316. Website: http://bronkonagurski.com/museum.htm.

**Voyageurs National Park,** 3131 US 53, International Falls. Call 218-283-6600. Website: www.nps.gov/voya.

**Waters of the Dancing Sky,** MN 11. Website: www.watersofthedancing sky.org.

## Dining

**Almost Lindy's,** Crystal Beach, International Falls. Call 218-286-3364. Website: www.almostlindys.com.

**Chocolate Moose Restaurant Company,** US 53 South, International Falls. Call 218-283-8888. Website: www.chocolatemooserestaurant.com.

**Coffee Landing,** 444 Third Street, International Falls. Call 218-283-8316.

**Giovanni's,** 301 Third Avenue, International Falls. Call 218-283-2600. Website: www.giosifalls.com.

**Grandma's Pantry,** 2079 Spruce Street, Ranier. Call 218-286-5584. Breakfast is the specialty, and it's served all day in gigantic portions, but the homemade sandwiches, soups, and dinners are tasty too.

## Other Contacts

**Boundary Waters Canoe Area Wilderness Permit Reservation Center,** 8901 Grand Avenue Place, Duluth. Call 218-626-4300. Website: www .bwcaw.org.

**Ely Chamber of Commerce,** 1600 East Sheridan Street, Ely. Call 218-365-6123; 800-777-7281. Website: www.ely.org.

**International Falls Convention and Visitors Bureau,** 301 2nd Avenue, International Falls. Call 800-325-5766. Website: www.rainylake.org.

**Lake Kabetogama Tourism Bureau,** 9903 Gamma Road, Lake Kabetogama. Call 800-524-9085. Website: www.kabetogama.com.

**Voyageurs National Park Association,** 126 North 3rd Street, Suite 400, Minneapolis. Call 612-333-5424. Website: www.voyageurs.org.

**Woody's Pub,** 3481 Main Street, Ranier. Call 218-286-5001; 855-410-5001. Website: http://fairlyreliable.com.

Roseau's Pioneer Village.

CHAPTER

5

# The Canadian Border: West to Roseau

**Estimated length:** 60 miles
**Estimated time:** 2 hours

**Getting there:** From the Twin Cities, take I-94 west to exit 178 and head northeast on MN 24 until you reach US 10. Follow US 10 to Little Falls, then follow MN 371 north to US 2 west. In Bemidji, turn onto US 71 north. From there, drive to MN 1 and turn left, turning right at MN 72 and follow that to MN 11 and Baudette.

**Highlights:** Fishing and boating on Lake of the Woods; the 3-mile beach at Zippel Bay State Park; historic Fort St. Charles; Roseau's Pioneer Village; bird-watching in Lost River State Forest.

The border lakes region was shaped by former glacial lakes and settled by Chippewa Indians, followed by French traders and eventually Scandinavians, looking for fertile farmland. People farm here still, but outdoor recreation is a favorite pastime of both residents and visitors. Part of the border boundary is the **Rainy River,** which flows from its source, Rainy Lake, on the eastern end of the border. Rainy River divides the United States and Canada right up to the point where it meets **Lake of the Woods,** an enormous lake stretching far north into Canada. This is one of the most remote spots in the state, and what it lacks in amenities, it makes up for in peaceful beauty.

The northwestern stretch of the state is geared primarily toward visitors who want to enjoy outdoor activities, including fishing (both summer and winter), boating, hiking, hunting, snowmobiling, snowshoeing, and cross-country skiing. Consequently, many resorts in this area are open year-round to cater to clients who favor activities in the different seasons. Note: because winter can be unpredictable, don't head out to this part of the state in the middle of January without a snow emergency kit in your vehicle, as well as a charged-up cell phone. Pay close attention to the weather, as snowstorms (complete with dangerous winds and wind chills) can arise quickly.

The lakes that punctuate the region are known for excellent fishing and boating. The fishing season has grown in popularity through increased technology in terms of the winter season; today many northern lakes are dotted by buildings ranging from little more than shacks to larger, heated buildings with attached Porta-Potties, known as sleepers, but all considered ice houses to be used for winter fishing. Ice fishing, combined with other winter sports such as cross-country skiing, snowmobiling, and snowshoeing, have made the northern region a year-round destination rather than a summer-only spot.

**Lake of the Woods** is one of the nation's largest lakes (after the Great Lakes and Salt Lake), and it's become a favored place of fishermen from all over the country and Canada. The region is proud of its walleye population, but there are many kinds of fish for the catching: lake sturgeon, northern pike, smallmouth and largemouth bass, perch, and muskie are just some of the plentiful fish. You can bring your own boat and manage your fishing yourself, or you can hire a guide through one of the many guide services (and through many of the dozens of resorts throughout the area) to assist you.

There is a separate summer and winter fishing season. Winter's ice fishing has gained considerable ground as more resorts offer ice houses for rent, many of which are outfitted with propane heaters and cooktops. The popularity of sleeper fish houses, outfitted like rustic cabins, also continues to grow. Fish spearing is another activity that is increasing in interest. Official seasons and regulations can be found through the Minnesota Department of Natural Resources (information at the end of this chapter).

Deer hunting in Minnesota begins in late October for bow hunters and early November for firearms. Besides deer hunting, duck, grouse, and goose hunting are all popular activities. Because there is so much open land near

Lake of the Woods, it's easy to mistake private property for public hunting grounds. Check with the local tourist offices or with your resort owners, who can provide necessary information to help you avoid trespassing. Minnesota DNR has specific licensing and regulation information. Many of the resorts in this area can recommend or are available for hire as hunting guides to help you maximize your time.

There are over 400 miles of snowmobile trails in the Lake of the Woods area, most groomed and maintained by a local snowmobiling organization, the **Lake of the Woods Drifters Snowmobile Club** (contact information at the end of this chapter). The Drifters can provide maps and trail conditions during the winter season. If you're going to be using the trails extensively, it's worth considering a membership in the Drifters (annual individual fee is $25, family rate is $35) in order to participate in one of the many events they sponsor during the snowmobiling season.

There are attractions and historical sites in this part of the state, but the emphasis here is outside, not inside.

You'll get your first taste of the favored local sport when you arrive in Baudette on MN 11, and **Willie Walleye** is there to greet you. No visit to the northern lakes would be complete without a photo op at the walleye

---

## GOLFING IN THE FAR NORTH

Golf's charm is felt this far north. There are several courses available to the public across the region:

**Oak Harbor Golf Course** in Baudette is a nine-hole course open May 1 to October 15, weather permitting.

**Oakcrest Golf Club** in Roseau is an 18-hole championship course that winds along the river and twists through the woods. Open mid-May to mid-October, weather permitting.

**Warroad Estates Golf Course** is an 18-hole course that straddles the U.S.–Canadian border. Open April 15 to October 15, weather permitting.

**Northwest Angle Country Club,** located at the farthest northern part of the contiguous United States: the **Northwest Angle.** When a golf course's location is described as "north of Northern Minnesota," you know you're truly going "up north." A nine-hole course that may not be the most pristinely groomed course you've ever played, but you may never be able to see quite so much wildlife while golfing, either. Open May through September, weather permitting.

*Willie Walleye.*

equivalent of Paul Bunyan. Forty feet long and weighing two tons, Willie represents Baudette's claim of being the "Walleye Capital of the World." (A claim, it should be noted, disputed by other popular walleye destinations in the state.)

The **Lake of the Woods County Museum** in Baudette is a small but well-stocked museum with exhibits on various aspects of northern Minnesota's history and development, including a re-created homestead kitchen, school, country store, and tavern, as well as information on the geology of the area.

The nicest hotel in Baudette itself is the Americinn, which offers rooms and suites, an indoor pool, cold-weather hook-ups, a fish-cleaning area, and free high-speed Internet access. Upgraded rooms include a fireplace. You can get a good meal at the **Ranch House** in Baudette. Three meals a day, all of them hearty. Burgers and ribs are the specialty.

North of Baudette on MN 172, where the Rainy River meets Lake of the Woods, you can find the **Border View Lodge.** This resort has several cabins, all of which are fully equipped and have the option of full daily maid service (bed making, dish washing). Border View also offers ice houses, both for daily use and for accommodation for that all-night ice fishing getaway. There's a bar and restaurant in the lodge. Not far away is the **Wigwam Resort.** The Wigwam offers both hotel rooms in the lodge and cabins for rental. Guests can book accommodations only, or they can reserve packages that include meals at the resort's restaurant and charter fishing with a guide.

Continue north on MN 172, which closely follows the shoreline of Rainy River up to Lake of the Woods. Turn west onto County Route 8 (CR 8), which will bring you to **Zippel Bay State Park.** Fishing, swimming, camping, bird-watching—Zippel Bay State Park offers these and more in its 3,000-plus acres along Lake of the Woods. Six miles of hiking trails during the summer are expanded to 11 miles in the winter for cross-country skiers. During the summer, get your fill of the vast Lake of the Woods by hiking along Zippel Bay State Park's 3-mile beach. Note: stop at one of the local gas stations and bait shops and ask what the best repellent is for deerflies, which can be a nuisance in the summer.

West of the park, near the town of Williams, is **Zippel Bay Resort.** Located right on Zippel Bay, this resort has both budget cabins and deluxe log cabins, complete with fireplace and Jacuzzi; the log cabins are attractive and spacious, located on the water's edge. The resort has an outdoor pool for the summer months and a restaurant. During the winter, make sure to spend some time at the **Zippel Igloo,** an on-ice "igloo" with several holes for fishing—and catered food and drinks, not to mention a satellite TV. Packages are available with or without meals; during the winter, sleeper ice houses can be rented.

If you want to venture out of your resort or cabin for food, you can stop by the **Williams Café** for plates full of home-cooked breakfasts and juicy burgers.

At this point, you can choose to continue west on CR 8 until you reach CR 17, then head south to return to MN 11 heading west to Warroad. Or, if you'd like to spend more time enjoying the view of the vast Lake of the Woods, you can take CR 53 (note: this is a gravel road) until you make a right turn on CR 51. Make an almost immediate left on CR 52 (also known as Sandy Shores Drive), and follow it north along the lakeshore to **Birch Beach.** Continue inland on CR 52 to MN 2, which will take you north to **Lude,** one of the northernmost spots in Minnesota that doesn't involve crossing international waters. From Lude, you will return down MN 2, making a right turn onto MN 11 and following that to MN 17. Take a left turn there and return to CR 11, traveling to **Warroad.**

In Warroad, **Fort St. Charles** is a worthy stop. In the early 1700s a French explorer and trader by the name of Pierre Gaultier de Varennes, Sieur de la Verendrye, established this fort as a base for trading and for launching expeditions. However, lack of food and hostility from local Sioux made the fort difficult to maintain, and it was abandoned after 1760. The buildings were discovered and reconstructed as a historical site in the mid-1900s.

Another worthwhile point of interest is the **Wm. S. Marvin Training and Visitor Center** at CR 11 and MN 313. The Marvin Visitor Center is a historic and industrial exhibition, featuring the growth and technology behind Marvin Windows and Doors. Theatrical highlights include an account of the fire that destroyed the Marvin plant in 1961 and how the Marvin company rebuilt and expanded. Tours of the Marvin plant itself are available by appointment at 218-386-4333, Monday through Friday only.

You might work up an appetite from all this sightseeing. **Izzy's Lounge and Grill** is a local bar and grill; the bar is fully stocked, and the grill provides enormous meals in the form of burgers and chicken. Service is friendly, and the casual environment, with a large stone fireplace, is downright cozy.

**Lakeview Restaurant,** just off CR 74 (also known as Lake Street NE), is a more upscale restaurant. Steak, shrimp, and burgers are served while diners enjoy a stellar view of the lake. Your after-dinner entertainment is taken care of too—the restaurant is located in the **Seven Clans Casino**.

Just outside the city of Warroad is the **Springsteel Resort & Marina.** Here you can reserve a cabin that's either on the lakeshore or tucked back into the woods. A restaurant and bar is on-site, and year-round fishing is available.

If you'd prefer a more unusual type of accommodation, right in Warroad itself is the **St. Mary's Motel Room.** Housed in the historic world's largest all-weather log church, the motel room is built into the former balcony and offers 22-foot-high ceilings and a Jacuzzi.

From Warroad, travel west on MN 11through the **Lost River State Forest** to reach **Roseau.** Lost River State Forest is an excellent stop for birders, with sightings including great gray owls, northern hawks, boreal chickadees, and magnolia warblers.

Roseau marks a transition point in terms of the environment. The large forests to the east begin to give way to the prairies of the Red River Valley in the west. The changing scenery also provides unique opportunities for spending time outdoors, as you can easily be deep within the forest and very quickly travel to prairie grasslands, seeing striking changes in flora and fauna along the way.

Roseau is also known as the birthplace of snowmobiles, and its history and current role in the world of snowmobiling are on display at the **Polaris Experience.** One of the leading manufacturers of snowmobiles, Polaris built this visitors center adjacent to its plant to showcase the company's history. The exhibits range from the earliest snowmobile prototypes to today's sleeker machines, as well as history and trivia from the age of snowmobiles. Tours of the Polaris plant itself are scheduled daily at 2 PM; call ahead or stop by the office to sign up. Admission is free.

Just west of Roseau is the **Pioneer Village.** This lovingly preserved village is a testament to the pioneer days of northwestern Minnesota's agricultural history. Most of the 16 buildings are restored artifacts, done primarily by volunteer labor (volunteer opportunities are available on

*The Polaris Experience, Roseau*

Tuesdays—call the village for more information). Visitors are welcome to explore on their own or take a guided tour through the post office, parish hall, church, barn, blacksmith shop, and log cabin. Bathroom facilities are, fittingly, the outhouse type—a vintage Porta-Potty.

Accommodations within Roseau itself are somewhat limited. The Americinn is one of the nicest hotels in Roseau, offering rooms and suites, an indoor pool, and cold-weather hook-ups. Nearby is the **North Country Inn and Suites,** a motel with 49 rooms and suites, all with refrigerators and microwaves, and daily continental breakfast. There is an indoor pool and hot tub as well.

For a good meal, check out the **Reed River Restaurant and Bar**, a full restaurant and bar located near the Polaris Experience. Reed River has burgers, sandwiches, steaks, and ribs. Or if you'd like to enjoy a more old-fashioned dining experience, check out **Earl's Drive In** for burgers and malts.

## IN THE AREA

### Accommodations

**Americinn Baudette,** MN 11 West, Baudette. Call 218-634-3200; 800-396-5007. Website: www.americinn.com.

**Americinn Roseau,** MN 11 West, Roseau. Call 218-463-1045; 800-396-5007. Website: www.americinn.com.

**Border View Lodge,** 3409 MN 172 NW, Baudette. Call 800-776-3474. Website: www.borderviewlodge.com.

**North Country Inn and Suites,** 902 3rd Street NW, Roseau. Call 888-300-2196. Website: www.northcountryinnandsuites.com.

**Springsteel Resort & Marina,** 38004 Beach Street, Warroad. Call 218-386-1000; 800-605-1001. Website: www.springsteelresort.net.

**St. Mary's Motel Room,** 202 Roberts Avenue NE, Warroad. Call 218-386-2474.

**Wigwam Resort,** 3502 Four Mile Bay Drive NW, Baudette. Call 218-634-2168; 800-448-9260. Website: www.wigwamresortlow.com.

*Zippel Bay Resort cabins.*

**Zippel Bay Resort,** 6080 39th Street NW, Williams. Call 800-222-2537. Website: www.zippelbay.com.

## Attractions and Recreation

**Fort St. Charles,** The Point, Lake Street NE, Warroad. Call 218-223-4611.

**Lake of the Woods County Museum,** 119 8th Avenue SE, Baudette. Call 218-634-1200. Website: www.lakeofthewoodshistoricalsociety.com/.

**Northwest Angle Country Club,** Angle Inlet. Call 218-223-8001. Website: www.pasturegolf.com/courses/nwangle.htm.

**Oak Harbor Golf Course,** 2805 24th Street NW, Baudette. Call 218-634-9939. Website: www.oakharborgolfcourse.com.

**Oakcrest Golf Club,** 5th Street South, Roseau. Call 218-463-3016. Website: www.oakcrestgolfcourse.com.

**Pioneer Village,** MN 11, Roseau. Call 218-463-3052. Website: www .roseaupioneerfarm.com.

**The Polaris Experience,** 205 5th Avenue SW, Suite 2, Roseau. Call 218-463-4999. Website: www.polarisindustries.com.

**Warroad Estates Golf Course,** 37293 Elm Drive, Warroad. Call 218-386-2025. Website: www.warroadestates.com.

**Willie Walleye,** Bayfront Park, Baudette.

**Wm. S. Marvin Training and Visitor Center,** Highways 11 and 313, Warroad. Call 218-386-4334. Website: www.marvin.com.

**Zippel Bay State Park,** CR 8, Williams. Call 218-783-6252. Website: www.dnr.state.mn.us/state_parks/zippel_bay/index.html.

## Dining

**Brickhouse Bar & Grille,** 205 5th Avenue SE, Roseau. Call 218-463-0993. A full restaurant and bar located near the Polaris Experience, Reed River has burgers, sandwiches, steaks, and ribs.

**Earl's Drive In,** 1001 3rd Street NE, Roseau. Call 218-463-1912.

**Izzy's Lounge and Grill,** 801 State Avenue North, Warroad. Call 218-386-2723. Website: www.patchmotel.com/izzys.htm.

**Lakeview Restaurant,** 1205 East Lake Street, Warroad. Call 218-386-1225. Website: www.sevenclanscasino.com/warroad.html.

**Ranch House,** 203 West Main Street, Baudette. Call 218-634-2420. Burgers and ribs.

**Williams Café,** 2335 94th Avenue NW, Williams. Call 218-783-3474. Home-cooked breakfasts and juicy burgers.

## Other Contacts

**Convention and Visitors Bureau of Roseau,** 121 Center Street East, Roseau. Website: goroseau.com

**Lake of the Woods Drifters Snowmobile Club,** Baudette. Call 218-634-3042. Website: www.lowdrifters.org.

**Lake of the Woods Tourism,** Baudette. Call 218-634-1174; 800-384-3474. Website: www.lakeofthewoodsmn.com

**Minnesota Department of Natural Resources.** Call 651-296-6157; 888-646-6367. Website for fishing information: www.dnr.state.mn.us/regulations/fishing/index.html. For hunting information: www.dnr.state.mn.us/regulations/hunting/index.html.

**Warroad Convention and Visitors Bureau,** Warroad. Call 218-386-3543; 800-328-4455. Website: www.warroad.org.

*Boat landing, Itasca State Park.*

CHAPTER

6

# Northern Lakes and Forests, Part 1:
## South from Bemidji

**Estimated length:** 130 miles
**Estimated time:** 5 hours

**Getting there:** From the Twin Cities, take I-94 west to exit 178 and head northeast on MN 24 until you reach US 10. Follow US 10 to Little Falls, then follow MN 371 north to US 2 west to Bemidji.

**Highlights:** The Art Walk in Bemidji; Itasca State Park; Dorset, the "Restaurant Capital of the World"; the Heartland Trail; Chippewa National Forest.

This is the area of Minnesota that is well known for something both enormous and tiny at the same time: the **headwaters of the Mississippi,** found in **Itasca State Park.** When you consider how mighty the Mississippi becomes even partway down Minnesota, let alone all the way to the Gulf of Mexico, it's amazing to see it as a gentle trickle that's easy enough to wade across. This is a densely forested part of the state, with large old-growth tracts of pine trees, as well as wetlands and hundreds of little lakes apparently around every corner. Lakes are even reflected in the name of one of the region's largest towns, **Bemidji,** which is Ojibwa for "lake with water flowing through." Many of the settlements here grew out of the logging industry, but today tourism is a major force for towns like Bemidji, **Park Rapids,** and **Walker.**

Bemidji is the county seat and home to Bemidji State University, located on the shores of Lake Bemidji. The downtown area is compact and includes several points of interest to visitors. The area's logging, pioneer, and Native American history is on display at the **Beltrami County History Center**. The History Center resides in the restored 1912 Great Northern Railway Depot, the last depot built by railroad baron James J. hill. The building's architecture itself is worth a visit, but the collection within is entertaining and enlightening, from Native American artifacts to a restored telegraph office. A separate research area offers historians access to archival materials.

Families are welcome at the **Headwaters Science Center.** Essentially a children's science museum, the HSC offers a variety of hands-on activities, as well as a collection of live animals (snakes, turtles, salamanders) for kids to learn about and handle.

The **Bemidji Community Art Center** is located in the historic Carnegie Library building on the lakeshore, which is listed on the National Register of Historic Places. Inside there are three galleries that display the work of national and regional artists, as well as hosting live music and poetry readings. New exhibits appear monthly from February through December. The Art Center also sponsors a series of First Fridays, which showcase art and live performances both in the center and around Bemidji.

Close to the lakefront is the **Paul Bunyan Playhouse.** With over 55 years of productions, this is one of the country's longest continuously operating summer stock theaters. The Paul Bunyan Playhouse uses both national professional actors as well as local talent for its summer season. Veterans of the Playhouse have gone on to professional theater careers in the Twin Cities.

The lakefront itself has several attractions. The **Bemidji Art Walk** is an outdoor sculpture garden curving along the shores of Lake Bemidji. Stop by the tourist information center on the lakefront and pick up a self-guided tour brochure to begin exploring the sculptures and murals that appear lakeside and into downtown.

A visit to Bemidji isn't quite complete without a photo opportunity near the statues of the legendary **Paul Bunyan and Babe the Blue Ox.** Besides, it's a good starting point for visiting the Art Walk. The statues are right by the **Paul Bunyan Amusement Park,** which is open every day in the summer, offering rides for small children and old-fashioned miniature golf.

## CONCORDIA LANGUAGE VILLAGES

North of Bemidji is **Concordia Language Villages.** Take US 71 north to County Route 20 (CR 20, also known as Birchmont Beach Road NE), turning right, then turn left at Thorsonveien NE to reach the campus. This renowned language school, headquartered in Moorhead, holds the majority of its classes and camps at an expansive site just outside Bemidji. The languages (including French, German, Spanish, Korean, Russian, Norwegian, and Swedish) are taught in villages, small towns created to resemble a town in the country of origin. Around one corner you'll find a beautiful German village; around the next, a colorful Spanish center. Most of the villages in Bemidji are centered near Turtle Lake, but a few are about 10 miles north. Each village is separate from the other; programs are offered for kids and adults. Even if you're not planning on learning a foreign language, visiting the villages for the beautiful sightseeing and loving re-creations of international villages makes this worth a stop.

The **Paul Bunyan Trail** winds around the east side of Lake Bemidji on its way to **Lake Bemidji State Park.** The park may not have the Mississippi headwaters, but it is a worthy stop, with acres of forest, access to Lake Bemidji for boating and fishing, a paved bike trail, and scores of birds for watching. The 110-mile Paul Bunyan Trail runs from Lake Bemidji State Park to Brainerd. It's a popular choice for bikers, and there are several bike-in campsites along the way, as well as bicycle rentals in many of the towns along the route.

Continue north on US 71 until you reach CR 15. Follow CR 15 north to find **Buena Vista Ski Village.** The mountains may not be the highest, but Buena Vista offers beautiful scenery to enjoy with its 16 runs. Cross-country skiing, tubing, snowboarding, and horse-drawn sleigh rides are all offered while there's snow. In the summer, the winter ski resort becomes **Buena Vista Ranch,** a logging village and visitor center during the summer months. Activities include covered wagon tours, horsemanship training clinics, and fall foliage rides. Reservations are recommended; call for information.

Bemidji has several lodging choices, mostly chains, but with a couple of exceptions. The **Hampton Inn** is right on Lake Bemidji, a short walk from the tourist information center and the beginning of the Art Walk. Full breakfast is included in the rates, and all rooms have high-speed Internet access. The hotel also has a Green Mill pizza restaurant for lunch and dinner. Near the **Paul Bunyan Mall** is the **Americinn Motel & Suites.** The Americinn offers 59 units, 26 of which are suites. The property has in indoor pool, whirlpool, and sauna, and the rates include continental breakfast. Also near the mall is the **Holiday Inn Express.** Most rooms have two queen beds, while a few upgraded rooms have king beds and Jacuzzi baths.

**Villa Calma Bed and Breakfast,** located near Lake Bemidji, offers four rooms, two with private bath and two with shared bath. All rooms have upgraded bed coverings and bathrobes, and full breakfast is included, as is an early-evening glass of wine. A common great room serves as the breakfast point, with lovely views of the lake, and the backyard has a fire pit and double hammock for guest relaxation. Villa Calma is also on the Paul Bunyan Trail.

Just outside town is a family resort that's something of a tradition on Lake Bemidji. Take US 71 to MN 97, then to CR 21 to find **Ruttger's Birchmont Lodge,** which offers both lodge and cabin accommodations. The Cedar Lodge offers the most luxurious suites, with lakefront setting and fireplaces, while the Main Lodge offers the more economical rooms. Cedar Lodge is open year-round, while the Main Lodge is open only in the summer. In addition, there are 22 cottages (mostly open only mid-May to Labor Day) and seven villas (larger than the cottages), which are open year-round. The resort has a restaurant and bar, which are open during the summer months. There is an indoor pool and hot tub, open all year, and boat and bike rental during the summer. A large sandy beach makes for a great summer resting spot, and during the summer Ruttger's offers a supervised kids' program for children ages 4 through 12.

Bemidji has a number of good restaurant options. **Peppercorn** is a steakhouse with a friendly staff and generous portions. Peppercorn's emphasis is on steak, ribs, and seafood. On Monday through Thursday nights the restaurant offers a rotating "all you can eat" selection, varying from crab legs to chicken and ribs. The food is good and the service is quick. The quintessential small-town bakery and café, **Raphael's Bakery Café** serves delicious breakfasts and lunches and sells baked goods to go. The menu may be limited (salads, sandwiches, soups) but the baked goods are pleasingly fresh, and the soups are homemade and worth buying extra for takeout. **Brigid's Cross** is a cheerful Irish pub with the usual suspects (fish and chips, ploughman's platter, shepherd's pie) and the not-so-Irish variations (macaroni and cheese bites, mini burger basket). The food is hearty, a full bar is available, and a variety of events is offered, from open mike to trivia contests to live music. **Keg & Cork** is a friendly neighborhood bar and grill. The locals love it, so you know it's good.

From Bemidji, take US 71 south to MN 200 west to reach **Itasca State Park/Mississippi headwaters.** This is Minnesota's oldest state park, and it's also well known for being the starting point of the Mississippi River (not to mention the point at which you can easily walk across the river). The quest to find the beginning of the Mississippi led explorers to various sites around the Bemidji area. But in 1832 Henry Schoolcraft, led by Anishinabe guide Ozawindib, found the true source. The name *Itasca* came from Schoolcraft's combining the Latin words for truth and head, *veritas* and

*Mississippi Headwaters, Itasca State Park.*

*caput*, into one word by using the letters in the middle. Later in the 19th century, the area that's now the park was in danger of being deforested by logging when surveyor Jacob Brower, alarmed at the loss of natural habitat, began an intense campaign in the state government to preserve the area. He succeeded—by one vote.

Today the headwaters is a major attraction, but it's just a small part of this 32,000-acre park. There 49 miles of hiking trails and 16 miles of paved biking trails include the 10-mile Wilderness Drive (road shared by bikes and cars), a winding, hilly stretch of road that meanders through the forests. To get a full view of the park, hike up to the top of the Aiton Heights Fire Tower, which you can reach from the Wilderness Drive. In the winter, trails are open for cross-country skiing, snowshoeing, and snowmobiling. You can rent bikes within the park, as well as boats, canoes, and fishing equipment.

Other sites to visit include the 500-year-old Indian cemetery and Wegmann's Cabin, a pioneer artifact. Conifers inhabit the Wilderness Sanctuary, a 2,000-acre stand of white and red pines, some upwards of 300 years old. The Bohall Wilderness Trail guides you through the pines and onto an overlook at Bohall Lake. There are campsites all through the park, but consider the option of staying at **Douglas Lodge**, located near Lake Itasca. The lodge was built in 1905 with timber from Itasca State Park and houses five guest rooms, a dining room, and a lounge. There is also a clubhouse that has rooms available, as well as several cabins.

Itasca State Park is by no means the only source for scenic lakes and trees in this part of the state. When you leave the Park, take MN 200 back to US 71 and turn south. You'll follow the edge of the park for a few miles, then past **Little Mantrap Lake**. Shortly after that, US 71 veers to the southeast, and you'll pass **Island Lake** and **Eagle Lake**. When you reach CR 40, turn left to enter an area crammed full of lakes surrounded by forests and rolling farmland. Follow CR 40 as it wanders east between Eagle Lake and **Potato Lake**, then turns south between Potato Lake and the aptly named **Blue Lake**. Take a right turn onto CR 4 and travel to south of **Ingram Lake**, then turn left onto CR 18. When CR 18 intersects with CR 7, turn left, and soon you'll be in **Dorset**.

Dorset may be small, but it's a great stop whether you're driving the back roads or enjoying the **Heartland State Trail**, which has a trailhead with parking in the village. The Heartland Trail is a 49-mile trail connecting Park Rapids to Cass Lake. Given the many lakes, wetlands, and

*Hiking trail, Itasca State Park.*

## DORSET: RESTAURANT CAPITAL OF THE WORLD

This tiny town has, tongue firmly in cheek, billed itself as the Restaurant Capital of the World, and certainly it's hard to believe any other town has as many restaurants per capita as this one does. With just 26 residents, Dorset has four restaurants, one for every 6.5 villagers. What's more surprising is that while the restaurants may not be profiled in *Food & Wine* anytime soon, they are worthy of a visit if you're in the neighborhood. Just follow the boardwalk down the main street (or take a detour from the Heartland Trail if you're out hiking or biking), and you'll find a good meal somewhere.

**Compañeros.** Americanized Mexican food served in cheerful abundance.

**Dorset Café.** This dinner-only café serves steaks and seafood and has a full bar.

**Dorset House Restaurant and Soda Fountain.** Choose from the buffet or from a pizza and burger menu; homemade pies and, of course, ice cream for dessert.

**LaPasta Italian Eatery.** Breakfast features include the standard pancakes and omelets, along with stuffed French toast and potato pancakes; lunch offers a few pasta items along with burgers and sandwiches; dinner is a changing roster of Italian foods.

woodlands along the trail, not only is it scenic, but it's a great place to explore the local wildlife. Deer, porcupines, beaver, muskrats, and occasional bobcats and coyotes all live in proximity to the trail.

Dorset is also home to the **Heartland Trail Bed and Breakfast,** a renovated 1920s community school building located on the Heartland Trail. The inn has five spacious guest rooms, all with private baths and fireplaces; full breakfast is served daily. Stay here, eat in the village, explore the Heartland Trail, and catch live performances nearby, either at the **Long Lake Theater** in Hubbard, a summer stock theater offering four to five productions each year along with holiday productions of *A Christmas Carol,* or at the **Northern Light Opera Company** in Park Rapids. The name of this company is a play on words; the "light" refers to "light opera" more than "northern lights." This grassroots organization has diligently been putting together productions, primarily of Gilbert and Sullivan, since 2001. Their success can be seen in their growth and in the branching out of their repertoire to include shows like *Into the Woods.* Also in Park Rapids is **Jaspers**

**Jubilee Theater,** a lively, family-friendly live show incorporating music, magic, juggling, yodeling, dancing, and comedy skits.

If you want something other than what Dorset has to offer for dining, Park Rapids has some unique alternatives. The **MinneSoda Fountain** falls in the category of "don't miss." With more than 80 years of service in the heart of this small town, this is a 17-stool confectionery. Leave the calorie counter at home. **Goose Crossing Food and Spirits** has a cozy fireplace for winter warmth and a unique copper tree in the center of the dining room, as well as goose sculptures outside. A standard menu includes the usual supper club items, such as steak and prime rib; an "Up North Favorites" menu has beef tips over rice and chicken-fried pork or steak (either is highly recommended).

From Dorset, travel back to CR 18 on CR 7 and head east. The road slips between **Belle Taine Lake** and **Shallow Lake** before merging with MN 34 in Nevis. It's just a short jaunt to **Akeley,** the home of the state's largest **Paul Bunyan statue,** as well as the **Woodtick Musical Theater.** Billing its show as similar to those in Branson, Missouri, the Woodtick Theater offers a musical variety show each summer that's appropriate for all ages. The music encompasses country, folk, bluegrass, and gospel, and is accompanied by a comedy show.

A good lodging choice here is the **Crow Wing Crest Lodge,** which has nineteen cabins on the **11th Crow Wing Lake**. Cabins vary from rustic to upscale. The lodge itself was built by the Red River Logging Company in 1898 as part of its logging operations. When the logging industry declined, the lodge changed hands and served a variety of purposes, including being a chicken farm and a girls' etiquette camp. The resort prides itself on its environmental stance as the proprietors recycle lake water, use no pesticides or herbicides, and use only all-natural cleaning products. Kids' activities are offered daily during the summer, that is, if they aren't entertained enough on the sandy beach with the beach toys, paddleboats, and kayaks, or on the playground or the fishing dock.

Continuing north on MN 34, you'll arrive in the town of **Walker,** on the shores of **Leech Lake.** This is a major fishing destination; Leech Lake has walleye, perch, crappies, pike, and largemouth and smallmouth bass. Of course, you don't have to fish to appreciate the lake; boating itself is a favored activity. The Heartland and Paul Bunyan Trails both run through here, and are popular with bikers and snowmobilers.

Walker and Leech Lake are part of the **Chippewa National Forest.**

With over 666,000 acres, Chippewa National Forest has ample opportunity for outdoor adventures. The forest has 160 miles of hiking trails and cross-country ski trails, 330 miles of snowmobiling trails, 23 developed campgrounds and 380 camping sites, and a sandy swimming beach. Three visitors centers have programs and information: Norway Beach, Cut Foot Sioux, and Edge of the Wilderness Discovery Center. For water fans, the forest holds two of Minnesota's five biggest lakes, and there are nine canoe routes across various rivers and Leech Lake (note: some of these routes are more treacherous than others; when planning a canoe trip, check with the Chippewa National Forest for recommendations based on your skill level). The forest also has the largest breeding population of bald eagles in the lower 48 states.

Walker has numerous lodging choices, from the standard hotel or motel to more unique options. Located on the lakeshore is **Chase on the Lake,** an upscale resort and spa complex with a well-regarded restaurant on-site. **Embracing Pines Bed and Breakfast,** outside Walker on CR 38, has three warmly appointed rooms. Guests also have use of the sauna, bikes, and canoes. Also on CR 38 is **Bailey's Resort on Leech Lake,** with nine cabins on the lake and boats and bikes available to rent. On the southern shore of Leech Lake is **Northland Lodge,** with 17 custom-built log homes that can accommodate 2 to 25 people and have whirlpool tubs and fireplaces.

There are also several good restaurants in the area. The **Boulders** is an upscale restaurant with a casual atmosphere, serving steak, salmon, lamb chops, even paella, which is beautifully prepared and served. A good "special occasion" choice. A more casual option is the **Lucky Moose Bar and Grill,** which is housed in a log building. The newly renovated **Ranch House Supper Club** is an old-fashioned supper club, with steaks and prime rib, plus all-you-can-eat specials each night. **Charlie's Up North** is a casual restaurant serving steaks, fish, and roasted chicken. In the summer, **Charlie's Boathouse** is right next door, essentially an open-air version of Charlie's wrapped around a bar built out of an old boat.

When you leave Walker, follow MN 200 north to **Laporte,** then turn south on MN 64 to visit **Forestedge Winery.** Forestedge produces wines from rhubarb, chokecherries, raspberries, and plums grown on-site and has won several awards for its innovative beverages. A wine-tasting room and shop is open May through December, and there's also a separate gift shop with arts and crafts items, particularly cooking items, that the winery's owners have collected around the country, and even made themselves.

From Forestedge, return to MN 200 on MN 64. Follow MN 200 to US 71 to return to Bemidji.

## IN THE AREA

### Accommodations

**Americinn Motel & Suites,** 1200 Paul Bunyan Drive NW, Bemidji. Call 218-751-3000; 800-396-5007. Website: www.americinn.com.

**Bailey's Resort on Leech Lake,** 33216 CR 38, Walker. Call 218-547-1464. Website: www.baileysresort.com.

**Chase on the Lake,** 502 Cleveland Boulevard, Walker. Call 218-547-7777. Website: www.chaseonthelake.com.

**Crow Wing Crest Lodge,** 31159 CR 23, Akeley. Call 218-652-3111; 800-279-2754. Website: www.crowwing.com.

**Douglas Lodge,** Itasca State Park. Call 866-857-2757. Website: www.stay atmnparks.com.

*Douglas Lodge in Itasca State Park.*

**Embracing Pines Bed and Breakfast,** 32287 CR 38, Walker. Call 218-224-3519. Website: www.embracingpines.com.

**Hampton Inn,** 1019 Paul Bunyan Drive South, Bemidji. Call 218-751-3600; 800-426-7866. Website: www.hamptoninn.com.

**Heartland Trail Bed and Breakfast,** Dorset. Call 218-732-3252. Website: www.heartlandbb.com.

**Northland Lodge,** 2802 Northland Lane NW, Walker. Call 800-247-1719. Website: www.andersonsleech-lake.com/northland/index.htm.

**Ruttger's Birchmont Lodge,** 7598 Bemidji Road NE, Bemidji. Call 218-444-3463; 888-788-8437. Website: www.ruttger.com.

**Villa Calma Bed and Breakfast,** 915 Lake Boulevard NE, Bemidji. Call 218-444-5554; www.villacalma.com.

## Attractions and Recreation

**Beltrami County History Center,** 130 Minnesota Avenue SW, Bemidji. Call 218-444-3376. Website: www.beltramihistory.org.

**Bemidji Art Walk,** lakefront, Bemidji. Call 218-759-0164; 800-458-2223, ext. 105.

**Bemidji Community Art Center,** 426 Bemidji Avenue, Bemidji. Call 218-444-7570. Website: http://bcac.wordpress.com.

**Buena Vista Ski Village and Ranch,** 19276 Lake Julia Drive NW, Bemidji. Call 218-243-2231; 800-777-7958. Website: www.bvskiarea.com.

**Chippewa National Forest,** 200 Ash Avenue NW, Cass Lake. Call 218-335-8600. Website: http://fs.usda.gov/chippewa

**Northern Lights Casino and Hotel,** 6800 Y Frontage Road NW, Walker. Call 800-252-7529. Website: www.northernlightscasino.com.

**Concordia Language Villages,** 8607 Thorsonveien NE, Bemidji. Call 218-586-8600; 800-450-2214. Website: www.concordialanguagevillages .org.

**Forestedge Winery,** 35295 MN 64, Laporte. Call 218-224-3535. Website: www.forestedgewinery.com.

**Headwaters Science Center,** 413 Beltrami Avenue, Bemidji. Call 218-444-4472. Website: www.hscbemidji.org.

**Heartland Trail,** Park Rapids. Website: www.dnr.state.mn.us/state_trails/heartland/index.html.

**Jaspers Jubilee Theater,** MN 34, Park Rapids. Call 218-237-4333. Website: www.jasperstheater.com.

**Lake Bemidji State Park,** 3401 State Park Road NE, Bemidji. Call 218-755-3843. Website: www.dnr.state.mn.us/state_parks/lake_bemidji/index.html.

**Long Lake Theater,** CR 6, Hubbard. Call 218-732-0099. Website: www.longlaketheater.net.

**Northern Light Opera Company,** 11700 Island Lake Drive, Park Rapids. Call 218-237-0400. Website: www.northernlightopera.org.

**Paul Bunyan Amusement Park,** lakefront, Paul Bunyan Drive N and 2nd Street, Bemidji.

**Paul Bunyan and Babe the Blue Ox,** lakefront, Bemidji. Daily. Website: www.visitbemidji.com/bemidji/paulbabe.html.

**Paul Bunyan Playhouse,** 314 Beltrami Avenue, Bemidji. Call 218-751-7270. Website: www.paulbunyanplayhouse.com.

**Woodtick Musical Theater,** MN 34, Akeley. Call 218-652-4200; 800-644-6892. Website: www.woodticktheater.net.

## Dining

**The Boulders,** 8363 Lake Land Trail NW, Walker. Call 218-547-1006. Website: www.thebouldersrestaurant.com.

**Brigid's Cross,** 317 Beltrami Avenue, Bemidji. Call 218-444-0567. A cheerful Irish pub. Website: www.brigidsirishpub.com.

*Charlie's Boathouse in Walker.*

**Charlie's Up North/Charlie's Boathouse,** 6841 MN 371 NW, Walker. Call 218-547-0222. Website: www.charliesupnorth.com.

**Compañeros,** Dorset. Call 218-732-7624. Website: www.companerosof dorset.com.

**Dorset Café,** Dorset. Call 218-732-4072.

**Dorset House Restaurant and Soda Fountain,** Dorset. Call 218-732-5556.

**Goose Crossing Food and Spirits,** 17789 MN 34 East, Park Rapids. Call 218-732-2700. Website: www.goosecrossing.com.

**Keg & Cork,** 310 Beltrami Avenue NW, Bemidji. Call 218-444-7600. A friendly neighborhood bar and grill.

**LaPasta Italian Eatery,** Dorset. Call 218-732-0275. Website: www.dorset-lapasta.com/lapasta.htm.

**Lucky Moose Bar and Grill,** 441 Walker Bay Boulevard, Walker. Call 218-547-3295. Website: www.luckymoosebargrill.com.

**MinneSoda Fountain,** 205 South Main, Park Rapids. Call 218-732-3240.

**Peppercorn's,** 1813 Paul Bunyan Drive, Bemidji. Call 218-759-2794. A steakhouse with a friendly staff and generous portions. Website: www .peppercornrestaurant.com.

**Ranch House Supper Club,** 9420 MN 371 Northwest, Walker. Call 218-547-1540. Old-fashioned supper club, with steaks and prime rib, plus all-you-can-eat specials each night.

**Raphael's Bakery Café,** 319 Bemidji Avenue, Bemidji. Call 218-759-2015. The quintessential small-town bakery and café. Website: www.gr8 buns.com.

## Other Contacts

**Destination Dorset,** Dorset. Website: www.dorsetmn.com.

**Leech Lake Tourism Bureau,** Walker. Call 800-735-3297. Website: www.leechlake.org.

**Park Rapids Chamber,** MN 71 South, Park Rapids. Call 218-732-4111; 800-247-0054. Website: www.parkrapids.com.

**Visit Bemidji,** Bemidji. Call 877-250-5959. Website: www.visitbemidji .com.

*The big black duck in Blackduck.*

CHAPTER

7

# Northern Lakes and Forests, Part 2:
## North and East of Bemidji

**Estimated length:** 180 miles
**Estimated time:** 7 hours

**Getting there:** From the Twin Cities, take I-94 west to exit 178 and head northeast on MN 24 until you reach US 10. Follow US 10 to Little Falls, then follow MN 371 north to US 2 west to Bemidji.

**Highlights:** The Forest History Center; Scenic State Park; the Joyce Estate; the Lost 40; the rolling, curving highways that take you through miles of forests and wetlands and around the countless lakes in the region.

The land north and east of Bemidji is a wilderness that is often underestimated and underexplored. Most of this area is contained in the **Chippewa National Forest** (see Chapter 6 for more information about the forest), and there are adjacent and overlapping state forests here too, including **Welsh Lake State Forest, Koochiching State Forest,** and **Blackduck State Forest.** This part of the state doesn't have as much to offer in terms of amenities like restaurants, mini-golf, or movie theaters as other areas do. But what it does have is breathtaking stretches of old-growth forests; wildlife and bird-watching in abundance; myriad opportunities for fishing, hiking, biking, snowshoeing, cross-country skiing, snowmobiling, or even just a wonderful day's drive to enjoy sunlight flashing through pine trees;

## A LAKE FULL OF FISH

A bit farther on US 2 and you'll start to see signs for **Lake Winnibigoshish,** or, as it's known locally, **Lake Winnie.** Lake Winnie is the fifth-largest lake in the state, and 95 percent of its shoreline is undeveloped, meaning there are long stretches of untouched forest and shoreline here, with resorts and other businesses fewer and farther between. Even better, the lack of development means the lake isn't fished out, but is teeming with walleye, perch, and pike. The Minnesota DNR uses Lake Winnie in its walleye restocking program, trapping and collecting wall-eye to repopulate other lakes around the state. Just off US 2 are **Nodak Lodge** and **Denny's Resort;** north of US 2 on County Route 91 (CR 91) you can find **McArdle's Resort, Four Seasons Resort,** and **Becker's Resort** on the south-western shore. The resorts are open year-round and offer plenty of help with fishing and hunting, and additional amenities like pools and playgrounds.

wildflowers in bloom; and the quiet you can only find in a remote part of the state.

From Bemidji, take US 2 east into Chippewa National Forest. Weather permitting, take a break at **Norway Beach,** a swimming area with a mile-long sandy beach and pristine waters on Cass Lake. The beach has tall pine trees as its backdrop, making it seem even more remote than it really is.

As US 2 heads away from Lake Winnie, you'll approach the city of **Grand Rapids.** From here, you'll explore the **Edge of the Wilderness Scenic Byway.** But before heading into that wilderness, consider taking time to visit the **Forest History Center,** south of the city at the junction of US 2 and US 169. The history center has a visitors center and a re-created turn-of-the-century logging camp with costumed characters for guides. Visitors can board a floating cook shack, climb a 100-foot fire tower, and crawl through a decayed log while learning about Minnesota's logging history. A trail system takes visitors through the forest and along the Mississippi River to see where, during the heyday of logging, the logs were sent down the river.

Along US 2 is the **Judy Garland Museum.** Judy Garland was born in Minnesota in 1922 and spent her first four years here. The house she lived in has been moved from its original street to a location on US 169, a busy highway across from Home Depot, which detracts slightly from the house's charm. Garland's home has been lovingly restored with considerable atten-tion to detail, and the curators have procured a wide variety of artifacts,

*Lakeside, Edge of the Wilderness Byway.*

including the carriage Dorothy rode in upon her arrival at Oz. The museum did have a pair of ruby slippers, but those were stolen in 2005, and it's clearly a theft that the community still grieves.

Just a few miles north on MN 38, which is the road for the Edge of the Wilderness Byway, you can choose to simply drive the 47 miles to Effie, which is enjoyable in and of itself, with the heavy forests and wetlands and, in the warm months, profusions of wildflowers. Although it is beautiful at any time of year, if you have the flexibility, make the journey in the fall, when the colors are spectacular.

But there are some deviations from MN 38 that are worth considering. Just north of Grand Rapids, at milepost 3.4, is the **Lind-Greenway Mine** on the southern shore of Prairie Lake. This former mine, on the edge of the Iron Range, left behind a 200-foot-tall mountain of rock and low-grade iron ore fragments, hued in the intense red-black of taconite. Visitors are welcome to select a fragment as a souvenir.

*Picnic area at Norway Beach.*

Resuming your northerly direction, you'll drive through the **Black Spruce/Tamarack Bog Habitat.** Lining both sides of the road, this habitat was formed sixteen thousand years ago when the last of the glaciers still existed. Spruce and tamarack tower over the road, and if you were to wander into the bog, you'd find the ground to be wet and spongy.

### JOYCE ESTATE HIKE

For a more adventurous detour—and a glimpse into a way of life long gone—turn right on CR 60 and drive several miles to Blue Water Lake Road, where you'll find a parking lot for the **Trout Lake-Joyce Estate Hiking Trail.** From the trailhead, the hike to the Joyce Estate is about 6 miles round-trip. The estate was built on the shores of Trout Lake between 1917 and 1935 by David Joyce, whose fortune was made in the logging industry. He built a massive complex out of native stone and lumber, with 40 buildings, a seaplane hangar, nine-hole golf course, and clubhouse. The caretaker's complex itself had 17 buildings. It's a fascinating place to explore how the wealthy lived decades ago in the woods.

## BIG BOG STATE RECREATION AREA

The Big Bog Recreation area has two parts, southern and northern. The southern part is a campground and cabin area, with sandy swimming beaches and fishing access. The northern part contains the **Big Bog** itself. The bog is a 500-square-mile peat bog, the largest in the lower 48 states. A mile-long environmentally sensitive boardwalk was careful constructed to do as little damage as possible, and now visitors can wander a mile into the bog, with interpretive signs explaining the sights on either side. Parts of the bog are overgrown with trees; other parts are wide-open wetlands. Depending on the season, you might spot some rare orchids, or even some carnivorous plants. It's a walk that finds beauty even in something as desolate as the bog.

*The boardwalk at Big Bog State Recreation Area.*

Another facet of the area's history is on display at the **Camp Rabideau National Historic Landmark,** one of the best preserved Civilian Conservation Corps projects in the country. You can take a guided tour, or you can go on your own; interpretive displays with detailed information are present throughout.

There are not a lot of towns along the southern end of the Edge of the Wilderness Byway, but as you continue north you'll drive through **Marcell,** built a century ago as a logging town and, unusual for most older logging towns, still operating as such. **Bigfork** also has its roots in logging but has developed into a tourist services town too.

The Byway ends in **Effie,** named after the community postmaster's daughter in 1903. After 47 miles of rolling, densely forested terrain, the landscape changes into gentler, more open farmland. This is a good stopping point for lunch, and the **Effie Café** has good diner food.

The next stage of the journey turns westward, following MN 1. This is a sparsely populated road that twists and turns, sometimes through thick forests, sometimes along wetlands and bogs, other times past farmland. The majority of this route takes you through Koochiching State Forest.

Once you reach US 71, you have some options. The first is to turn south on US 71 and return to Bemidji (with a few suggested stops along the way). The second is to continue west on MN 1 to **Northome,** then travel north on MN 72 to **Waskish,** where you can visit the **Big Bog State Recreation Area** (see sidebar).

On your way to the Big Bog, you can take in a bit of local humor by stopping at the **Paul Bunyan Memorial Park** in Kelliher to pay respects to Paul himself—his enormous "grave" is right alongside the road, with a headstone that reads, HERE LIES PAUL AND THAT'S ALL. In the summer, you can take a break at the **Road Runner Drive-Inn** for a burger and shake.

The other option at the junction of MN 1 and US 71 is to turn south on MN 46 to Alvwood, then drive east on CR 29. Once you reach CR 26, turn

*Sunset over MN 1.*

north and drive to Forest Road 2240. Shortly after starting on the Forest Road, you'll come to the parking lot for the **Lost 40 Scientific and Natural Area (SNA)**. The Lost 40, which is actually 144 acres, is a tract of land that was accidentally misidentified as a lake by a surveyor during the logging boom times. Consequently, it remained untouched when forests around it were decimated. There are pine trees that are more than three hundred years old in the Lost 40, and wildflowers are prolific in the late spring. A 1-mile hiking trail guides you through this special and beautiful SNA.

The remaining stretch of this journey continues south on US 71, through towns as tiny as **Funkley** (population 15) to larger towns like **Blackduck** (which has not just one, but two large black duck statues, one on the highway and the other in the town's center). You can stop for a bite to eat at the **Countryside Restaurant,** where you can get a solid sandwich or burger.

Another spot for a good burger is the **Got-r-Dunn** in **Tenstrike,** a few blocks east of US 71. The burgers are hand formed and well seasoned. Or if you'd like an alternative to sandwiches and burgers, go a bit farther south on US 71 to **Turtle River** and stop at **Turtle River Pasties.** Made on the premises with all-butter crusts and house-cured meats, you can get them to eat there or to go, heated or frozen. You might want to pick up a few to bring home.

## IN THE AREA

### Accommodations

**Becker's Resort,** 17048 Wild Rice Drive, Bena. Call 218-665-2268. Website:www.beckersresort.com.

**Denny's Resort,** 15017 16th Avenue NE, Bena. Call 218-665-2222. Website: www.dennysresort.com.

**Four Seasons Resort,** 925 River Drive NW, Bena. Call 218-665-2231. Website: www.fishingwinnie.com.

**McArdle's Resort,** 1014 West Winnie Road NW, Bena. Call 218-665-1006; 800-535-2398. Website: www.mcardlesresort.com.

**Nodak Lodge,** 15080 Nodak Drive, Bena. Call 218-665-2226; 800-752-2758. Website: www.nodaklodge.com.

## Attractions and Recreation

**Big Bog State Recreation Area,** MN 72, Waskish. Call 218-647-8592. Website: www.dnr.state.mn.us/state_parks/big_bog/index.html.

**Edge of the Wilderness Scenic Byway.** Website: www.edgeofthewilderness.com.

**Forest History Center,** 2609 CR 76, Grand Rapids. Call 218-327-4482; 888-727-8386. Website: www.mnhs.org.

**The Judy Garland Museum,** 2828 US 169 South, Grand Rapids. Call 800-664-5839. Website: www.judygarlandmuseum.com.

*Paul Bunyan's "Grave," Kelliher.*

**Lost 40 Scientific and Natural Area (SNA),** Forest Road 2240, Chippewa National Forest. Website: www.dnr.state.mn.us/snas/sna01063/index .html.

**Paul Bunyan Memorial Park,** MN 72, Kelliher. Call 218-647-8470. Website: www.northernminnesota.org/destinations/db.htm?state=view_ site;id=3787.

## Dining

**Countryside Restaurant,** MN 72, Blackduck. Call 218-835-3333.

**Effie Café,** 100 NW CR 5, Effie. Call 218-743-3607.

**Got-r-Dunn,** 189 Main Street, Tenstrike. Call 218-586-3555.

**Road Runner Drive-Inn,** MN 72, Kelliher. Call 218-647-8717.

**Turtle River Pasties,** 12486 US 71, Turtle River. Call 218-586-4004. Website: www.summerkitchensupplies.com.

## Other Contacts

**Chippewa National Forest.** Website: www.fs.usda.gov.

**Grand Rapids Chamber of Commerce,** One NW Third Street, Grand Rapids. Call 218-326-6619; 800-472-6366. Website: www.grandmn.com.

*Grand View Lodge, Nisswa.*

CHAPTER

8

# Brainerd Lakes:
## Gull Lake and Environs

**Estimated length:** 120 miles
**Estimated time:** 6 hours

**Getting there:** From the Twin Cities, take US 169 north to Onamia.

**Highlights:** Lake Mille Lacs; the Pequot Lakes Fire Tower; the little town of Nisswa; the grand lodges of Brainerd.

If lakes are what people think of when they think about Minnesota, it's likely that they're thinking about the Central Lake District, particularly the Brainerd area. Slightly more than two hours north of the Twin Cities, these lakes have long been a popular summer weekend getaway spot, where a community of mom-and-pop resorts and upscale enclaves caters to all types of interests. Brainerd and its twin city of Baxter are the most prominent communities, but they are not the only cities to consider when looking at a lake vacation; many of the small towns surrounding Brainerd, including Nisswa, Pequot Lakes, and Crosslake. are good bets.

But beyond the Brainerd region are more good options for water enthusiasts. Minnesota's second-largest lake, **Lake Mille Lacs,** located east of Brainerd, is also an idyllic area for visitors. Both areas are blessed with natural beauty in abundance, plenty of outdoor recreational opportunities, and historic sites to visit.

*Lake Mille Lacs.*

Because these popular lake regions are close enough to the Twin Cities to enable weekend trips, traffic can be heavy, especially on weekends. The route to Brainerd has been improved by the addition of traffic lanes on MN 371, but Brainerd and Baxter are not towns designed for heavy traffic flow; be prepared for slow going at times.

Located on the Mille Lacs Reservation, Lake Mille Lacs is just about as popular in winter as it is in summer, thanks to a continually growing interest in ice fishing. The region has responded by adding more options for ice-house rental, including some very deluxe buildings with electricity and heat. Year-round, the outdoor options seem almost endless: fishing, hunting, boating, biking, hiking, cross-country skiing, snowshoeing, snowmobiling—it's all here, along with spectacular sunrises and sunsets. Note: US 169 is the main route along the lake, but periodically a frontage road will scoot closer to Mille Lacs for a stretch before merging back with US 169. Even though the two roads are close together, the frontage road gets you that much closer to the lake itself and is worth slowing down for.

## THOUSANDS OF YEARS OF HISTORY

**Mille Lacs Kathio State Park** is a National Historic Landmark because of the significant archaeological discoveries that have been made here. The Dakota people settled here hundreds of years before Europeans arrived, and pieces of copper tools found here have been dated back nine thousand years. By the 18th century, the Ojibwa were moving into the area too, and still live around Mille Lacs. The park's visitors center covers various stages in the region's history and heritage.

But as with any state park, the outdoors is as important. The Rum River flows through the park from its source in Lake Mille Lacs, and visitors can use canoes or rowboats to explore. A swimming beach is open during the summer, as is a 100-foot observation tower and a wide variety of campsites and cabins (some of which are year-round). There are 35 miles of hiking trails and 27 miles of horseback trails, both winding through second-growth stands of birch, maple, and oak trees. Winter enthusiasts can cross-country ski, snowshoe, or snowmobile on groomed trails. Among the types of wildlife frequently seen are hawks, owls, deer, beavers, and eagles.

**Mille Lacs Wildlife Management Area** is a small, carefully preserved WMA (61 acres) of forests and wetlands. During hunting season, camping is allowed and hunters with permits can hunt deer, bear, and small game.

There are other kinds of activities in the area besides the nature kinds. **Grand Casino Mille Lacs** is a full-scale gambling complex with slots, blackjack, and bingo. The complex also has several restaurants, a hotel, a theater with frequent live performances, a Kids Quest child-care area, and an extensive video arcade.

The **Mille Lacs Indian Museum,** near Mille Lacs Kathio State Park, is a joint venture between the Mille Lacs Band and the Minnesota Historical Society, and it's a thoughtful, detailed collection of exhibits showing how Native Americans of the region lived and worked centuries ago. The crafts room has an especially lovely collection of beadwork and birch-bark basketry. An adjacent trading post is a re-creation of a 1930s-era trading post and is open year-round on weekends to sell Native American gift items.

The Mille Lacs area is heavily geared toward the outdoorsman, with many resorts offering camping and cabins, along with boat rentals and fishing assistance. But there are some more upscale options as well. **Izatys Resort** is a luxury complex of townhouses and villas (ranging from two to four bedrooms), as well as a lodge offering hotel rooms on the shores of Lake Mille Lacs. Boat rental, two 18-hole golf courses, fishing and hunting guides, tennis courts, and indoor and outdoor pools are all available on-site, as is a well-regarded fine-dining restaurant. **Grand Casino Mille Lacs** has several room types, including a number of luxurious suites with four-person Jacuzzis and separate living areas. The large indoor swimming pool and whirlpool are in a nicely decorated wing. The casino has four restaurants on-site, one of which (Plums, a quick-service burger-and-pizza café) is open 24 hours Wednesday through Sunday. There's also a buffet restaurant, a casual grill restaurant, and a steakhouse open for dinner only. **Mille Lacs Lodge** is a rustic, cozy lodge with just six rooms. They can be rented individually or a group can rent the entire lodge at a discount from the individual room rate. All rooms have private baths. The lodge grounds have a covered picnic area and a fire pit; hunting and fishing guides can be arranged, as can home-cooked meals. **Twin Pines Resort** is the quintessential family-friendly resort with cabins and motel rooms on Lake Mille Lacs, and a restaurant and bar open all day. The property is a good value, with summer and winter fishing guides available (as well as icehouse rental in the winter) and a restaurant/bar on-site.

Outside the hotel dining realm is **Svoboda's Spotlite.** Breakfast is served all day at this friendly café, a local institution. The home-cooked foods are simple but delicious, and prices are reasonable.

Just past Garrison on the northwestern edge of Lake Mille Lacs, US 169 veers north. Stay on US 169 until you reach County Route 11 (CR 11) heading west. At this point, you're moving toward the Brainerd Lakes area, and you'll be winding your way past several smaller lakes and through wooded areas. Sure, there are faster ways to get from point A to point B, but they're not nearly as scenic! CR 11 winds along the south shore of **Farm Island Lake** before reaching **Bay Lake.** (Note: you cross county lines en route, so CR 11 becomes CR 14.) Take CR 6 north to Deerwood, where you'll connect with MN 210, driving in an appropriately sinuous manner around **Serpent Lake** to **Crosby.** Besides its lakeside location and opportunities for outdoor adventures, another reason to stop here is to book a room at the **Nordic Inn Medieval Brew & Bed.** Housed in a former Methodist church, the Nordic Inn has five rooms with disparate themes, including Odin's Loft, decorated with armor and weapons, and the Locker Room, decorated for Minnesota Vikings football fans. Breakfast is included in the room rates. On nights when enough rooms are occupied, guests can participate in an interactive Viking dinner theater performance, complete with Viking feast.

Driving into the Brainerd Lakes area, you're coming into one of the earliest major resort areas outstate. Nineteenth-century logging took a toll on this region, so by the end of that century the loggers were leaving, and entrepreneurial residents made good use of the area's myriad lakes, sandy beaches, and excellent hunting and fishing to establish the communities around Brainerd as a vacation idyll. The little towns of **Nisswa, Breezy Point, Pequot Lakes, Merrifield, Crosslake,** and **Lake Shore** established themselves as hospitable bases to enjoy all that the region has to offer.

Take MN 6 north to CR 36 west, driving through **Crow Wing State Forest** and **Cross Lake Game Refuge** and around **Square Lake** and **Velvet Lake.** CR 36 ends at **Tiff Lake.** From that point, travel north on CR 66 to **Crosslake** on the shores of **Cross Lake** (no, that's not a typo—the town is one word, the lake two). Crosslake has an interesting historic exhibit at the **Historic Log Village** on CR 66. The Log Village is a collection of

*The Historic Log Village, Crosslake.*

original log buildings transplanted to this corner and available for tours in the summer.

From Crosslake, travel south on CR 3 to CR 11 west, which runs along the northern border of **Pelican Lake** before turning south to **Breezy Point.** This small lakeside town is home to **Breezy Point Resort.** Located on Pelican Lake, this resort has a huge variety of accommodations to choose from—lodge rooms, one- and two-bedroom apartments, and a series of lodgings called Unique Retreats: log cabins, A-frame cabins, and full houses. For recreation, there are two 18-hole golf courses, an indoor pool, and an extensive sandy beach with boat rentals available. The summer months bring live musical performances. Winter brings a new round of activity, including a 9-hole golf course on the lake, skating rinks, cross-country skiing (equipment available for rental), and a snow tubing hill adjacent to the resort. The resort has two full-service dining areas, the most attractive of which is the Antlers Dining Room, which was built with post-and-beam construction and features two large antler chandeliers.

Continue westward on CR 11 to **Pequot Lakes.** As you approach the town, you'll see signs directing you to the **Pequot Lakes Fire Tower.** A short but steep hike takes you through dense woods to a hill that leads to this 100-foot tower. Definitely not for the faint of heart or weak of knees, but if you'd like a spectacular view of the surrounding forestland, you can climb the tower itself.

The **Paul Bunyan Trail** (see Chapter 6 for more information about the trail) runs right through town in a north–south direction. Pequot Lakes also has a good selection of shopping and restaurants available. You can grab a bite to eat at the **Tiki Room,** an oddly themed café that nevertheless has good deli food (especially good is the roast turkey and cranberry sauce sandwich on cranberry wild rice bread). The Tiki Room is in a small complex called the **Jack Pine Center,** which also features the **Brambleberry Jam and Jelly Co.,** a shop featuring locally grown and produced food products. The **A-Pine Family Restaurant** has been around for years, catching attention with its distinctive A-frame building. For something more substantial, check out the **Timberjack Smokehouse & Saloon.**

Traveling south on MN 371, you'll arrive in **Nisswa,** tucked along the southern edge of **Nisswa Lake** near **Roy Lake,** and not far from the northern edge of **Gull Lake.** Even though it's close to the Brainerd/Baxter area, it's quieter and still has the feel of a small village. The Heartland Trail and Paul Bunyan Trail are nearby.

## ANTIQUING

If you enjoy antiquing, Pequot Lakes has some browse-worthy shops.

**Beautiful Antiques,** 30960 Government Drive

**Castoffs,** 4242 Jokela Drive

**The Flour Sack Antiques Shop,** 29119 MN 371

**Mercantile Cooperative,** 30924 Government Drive

If you'd like to explore a little more in the antiques realm, you might want to detour slightly here and go a few miles north on MN 371 to **Jenkins,** a very small town, but with a crowded antique store right on the highway.

You can also get a taste of history at the **Nisswa Pioneer Village.** The Pioneer Village is comprised of nine buildings, including log homes and a schoolhouse, while the old caboose and train depot holds railroad relics. An annual Scandinavian festival attracts large crowds.

Less historic but just as fun (if not more) are the annual **Nisswa Turtle Races.** No worries about breakneck speeds in these races, held every Wednesday, rain or shine, in the summer months. Nevertheless, they're immensely popular with kids, and participation can rise into the hundreds. If you don't have your own turtle, it's possible to rent one. Races start at 2 PM.

Just south of Nisswa's Main Street is **Grand View Lodge.** Grand View hearkens back to the grand old days of lake resorts. Built in 1919, this venerable resort has maintained its historic elegance while modernizing with the amenities today's resort travelers want. The resort offers lodge rooms, cabins, and suites and villas on the property's golf course. An indoor pool and water slide shares a building with a fitness center, but in good weather swimming is done at the sandy beach. Boats can be rented, as can bikes and horses for riding. There are three 18-hole golf courses and one 9-hole course. The full-service spa is open year-round, as are the resort's six restaurants. Two separate kids' clubs, one for ages 3 to 6 and the other for ages 7 to 12, give parents a break from full-time child care.

In the neighboring community of Lake Shore, you can find **Lost Lake Lodge.** This small but lovely seasonal resort has beautifully outfitted cabins in a quiet, tucked-away location on Lost Lake. Rates are all-inclusive, meaning guests have full breakfast and four-course dinners daily included in their rates, and the food is well worth it (dinner is available to the public). Canoes, fishing boats, and bikes are also included in the rates,

## NISSWA SQUARE SHOPS

One of the most fun things to do in Nisswa is just while away a few hours visiting the shops along Main Street in a little shopping area called **Nisswa Square.**

**Rainy Days**. A bookseller for book lovers, with a wide range of reading material for grownups and for kids.

**Totem Pole**. All Minnetonka moccasins, all the time.

**Blue Canoe Boutique**. Casual and elegant clothing and jewelry.

**Simpler Thymes of Nisswa**. A gift shop focused on personal luxuries, including lotions and soaps, candles, gourmet foods (many locally produced), robes, and women's accessories.

**The Chocolate Ox**. A shop full of sugary temptations, from higher-end truffles to vintage candies and kiddie favorites.

**Adirondack Coffee**. A warm and cozy coffee shop that also retails its roasted-on-site coffee products.

**The Fun Sisters Boutique**. Fun indeed—a shop full of inexpensive accessories and makeup for girls of all ages.

**Lundrigans Clothing**. Casual but high-quality men's and women's clothing for the north woods lifestyle.

---

and fishing guides as well as massage therapists can be hired at an additional fee.

Just a few miles south of Nisswa on MN 371 is the **Brainerd Lakes area.** Brainerd is a town that had a rapid-fire start to its history. In 1870, when the railroad arrived, it consisted of a lone trading post. Along with rail came the loggers, for whom the railway was a necessity, and the town's growth was explosive. By the time the loggers left, tourism had already created an economic base that has continued to flourish, not surprising given the hundreds of lakes in close proximity to the town of Brainerd (and its twin, the city of Baxter).

Arguably one of the most popular lake areas in the state, the Brainerd Lakes area has undergone a shift over the last several years. The small-town community with a few large resorts and dozens of small mom-and-pop resorts is evolving into a larger-scale resort community, complete with more lodging, restaurants, and off-the-lake entertainment activities. The small resorts are still there, and thriving, as are the grander old-style hotel resorts, but they're being supplemented with newer chain hotels, including some that have amenities like indoor water parks. The increased efforts to bring in more traffic year-round have succeeded, and that means the area is perhaps not as restful as some of the other resort areas. That said, for visitors wanting a wider variety of options for their vacations, the Brainerd area is hard to beat.

As you start driving into Brainerd, you'll see **Pirate's Cove Mini-Golf** and the **Billy Bones Raceway** on the left side of MN 371 north. Pirate's Cove is a well-maintained and fun pirate-themed mini-golf course. You can play one of the two 18-hole courses, or play both at a discount. Next door is the Billy Bones Raceway, which has three go-cart tracks. Another form of entertainment can be found at **This Old Farm Pioneer Village and Paul Bunyan Land** on MN 18. It's part history village, part amusement park, with attractions like a 26-foot-tall talking Paul Bunyan, amusement rides, and the Pioneer Village, which includes an original log cabin, dentist's office, school house, and post office. Or, for more intense thrills check out one of Brainerd's most famous attractions: **Brainerd International Raceway**. Drag racing and road racing at its finest. Paul Newman has been among the racing participants.

For a more serious look at the area, the **Crow Wing County Historical Museum** is a lively museum that used to be the sheriff's office and county jail. Now it houses a wide-ranging collection of historical items detailing the region's lumber, railroad, and mining history, as well as Native American artifacts.

In the midst of the strip-mall highway landscape, the **Northland Arboretum** gives a taste of the nature that can be found outside the town. Rather incongruously located behind the Westgate Mall in Brainerd, this nature preserve covers 500 acres of forest and prairie that have evolved on the site of a former landfill. Open year-round, it has several miles of hiking and cross-country ski trails.

A final stop for this route is just south of Brainerd on MN 371: **Crow Wing State Park**. This is not only a pristine state forest, but a remnant of the area's past as a fur-trading hotbed. The town of Crow Wing flourished during the area's heyday, but when the railroad decided to pass through Brainerd rather than Crow Wing, the town's fate was sealed. Today the nearly 2,100-acre park has several miles of hiking trails (some of which are groomed for cross-country skiing in the winter) and excellent canoeing opportunities, including a canoe-in campsite. Within the park is the Beaulieu House, the last remaining building from the fur trading days.

*Crow Wing State Park.*

Lodging runs the gamut from small mom-and-pop cabin resorts to big elaborate full-service complexes. **Cragun's Resort** falls into the latter category. Besides the beautifully appointed rooms, cabins, and reunion houses, Cragun's has a 22,000-square-foot indoor sports complex with tennis and basketball courts, a running track, and a fitness center. The hotel itself has an indoor pool. A full-service spa is on-site. There are three restaurants that are open year-round, plus two more open in the summer. Fifty-four holes of golf will keep golfers happy, while boaters and fishing aficionados have direct access to Gull Lake (note: Cragun's does not allow personal watercraft, or jet-skis, to be stored or launched from their property). Bikes can be rented, and snowmobiles can be hired during the winter.

Next door to Cragun's is **Madden's,** another of the state's largest and nicest resorts, offerings rooms, cabins, and reunion houses. Three 18-hole golf courses are on the property, along with one 9-hole social course. Fishing, boating, hiking, swimming, and tennis are all offered, as is trapshooting (with one week's notice) and seaplane certification. A full-service spa is on-site, as is a children's program from July through mid-August for kids ages 4 to 12. There are seven restaurants, three fine dining and four casual.

**Ruttger's** has been welcoming guests since 1898, and is now a massive complex with condos, villas, cottages, lodge rooms, and a vacation house. There's an abundance of activities, from golf and fishing to spa services, a kid's camp, and even a high ropes course. Three restaurants on-site provide every culinary desire.

A newer resort is the **Lodge at Brainerd Lakes.** Opened in 2005, the lodge has sizable rooms and suites (including a Cinema Suite, featuring a 64-inch surround-sound, flat-screen TV), and it also reflects the newer generation of resorts with its 30,000-square-foot indoor water park, complete with tube and body slides, zero-entry pool, and indoor/outdoor hot tub.

For something completely different—but very family friendly and wonderfully tranquil—travel north of Brainerd on CR 4 to **Train Bell Resort.** There are several well-maintained lakeside cabins as well as a condo complex, but the resort still keeps its cozy feeling, assisted by weekly activities such as a pancake breakfast, minnow races, and Friday night dances. Fishing boats are available for rental, and kayaks and paddleboats at the sandy beach are included with the accommodations.

There are plenty of dining options too. A popular family choice is the **371 Diner**, right on US 371. The 371 Diner is a replica of a '50s diner and has a respectable (if high-calorie) menu of burgers, sandwiches, and ice cream treats. Kids' meals are served in a cardboard racecar. Close to the diner is the **Black Bear Lodge and Saloon,** which serves standard bar and grill fare, including sandwiches and burgers, steaks, and seafood. **Prairie Bay Grill** offers pizza, pasta, sandwiches, and "meat and potato" dishes, served in a casual yet upscale environment. Kids are welcome, as are vegetarians, who have several options on the menu.

In the older downtown of Brainerd is the **Sawmill Inn.** It doesn't look like much on the outside, but the Sawmill is the classic small-town café, complete with huge breakfasts and hearty sandwiches.

# IN THE AREA

## Accommodations

**Breezy Point Resort,** 9252 Breezy Point Drive, Breezy Point. Call 800-432-3777. Website: www.breezypointresort.com.

**Cragun's Resort,** 11000 Craguns Drive, Brainerd. Call 800-272-4867. Website: www.craguns.com.

**Grand Casino Mille Lacs,** 777 Grand Avenue, Onamia. Call 800-468-3517. Website: www.grandcasinomn.com.

**Grand View Lodge,** 23521 Nokomis Avenue, Nisswa. Call 218-963-2234; 866-801-2951. Website: www.grandviewlodge.com.

**Izatys Resort,** 40005 85th Avenue, Onamia. Call 800-533-1728. Website: www.izatys.com.

**The Lodge at Brainerd Lakes,** 6967 Lake Forest Road, Baxter. Call 218-822-5634; 877-687-5634. Website: www.lodgehotelsbrainerd.com.

**Lost Lake Lodge,** 7965 Lost Lake Road, Lake Shore. Call 218-963-2681; 800-450-2681. Website: www.lostlake.com.

**Madden's,** 11266 Pine Beach Peninsula, Brainerd. Call 218-829-2811; 800-642-5363. Website: www.maddens.com.

**Mille Lacs Lodge,** 8673 340th Street, Onamia. Call 320-532-3384. Website: www.millelacslodge.com.

**Nordic Inn Medieval Brew and Bed,** 210 First Avenue NW, Crosby. Call 218-546-8299. Website: www.vikinginn.com.

**Ruttger's Bay Lake Lodge,** 25039 Tame Fish Lake Road, Deerwood. Call 218-678-2885; 800-450-4545. Website: www.ruttgers.com.

**Train Bell Resort,** 21489 Train Bell Road, Merrifield. Call 800-252-2102. Website: www.trainbellresort.com.

**Twin Pines Resort,** 7827 US 169, Garrison. Call 320-692-4413; 800-450-4682. Website: www.twinpinesmillelacs.com.

*Twin Pines Resort, Lake Mille Lacs.*

## Activities and Recreation

**Billy Bones Raceway,** 17944 State Highway 371, Brainerd. Call 218-828-4245. Website: wwwbillybonesraceway.com.

**Blue Canoe Boutique,** 25497 Main Street, Nisswa. Call 218-963-7330.

**Brainerd International Raceway,** 5523 Birchdale Road, Brainerd. Call 218-824-7220; 866-444-4455. Website: www.brainerdraceway.com.

**The Chocolate Ox,** Main Street, Nisswa. Call 218-963-4443. Website: www.thechocolateox.com.

**Crow Wing County Historical Museum,** 320 Laurel Street, Brainerd. Call 218-829-3268. Website: www.crowwinghistory.org.

**Crow Wing State Park,** 3124 State Park Road, Brainerd. Call 218-829-8022. Website: www.dnr.state.mn.us/state_parks/crow_wing/index.html.

**The Fun Sisters Boutique,** 5380 Merill Avenue, Nisswa. Call 218-961-0071. Website: www.thefunsisters.com.

**Historic Log Village,** CR 66, Crosslake. Call 218-692-4056. Website: www.crosslakehistoricalsociety.org.

**Mille Lacs Indian Museum,** 43411 Oodena Drive, Onamia. Call 320-532-3632. Website: www.mnhs.org/places/sites/mlim.

**Mille Lacs Wildlife Management Area,** 29172 100th Avenue, Onamia. Call 320-532-3537. Website: www.dnr.state.mn.us/wmas/index.html.

**Mille Lacs Kathio State Park,** 15066 Kathio State Park Road, Onamia. Call 320-532-3523. Website: www.dnr.state.mn.us/state_parks/mille_lacs_kathio/index.html.

**Lundrigans Clothing,** 25521 Main Street, Nisswa. Call 218-963-2647. Website: www.lundrigansclothing.com

**Nisswa Pioneer Village,** Main Street, Nisswa. Call 218-963-0801.

**Nisswa Turtle Races,** Nisswa Trailside Information Center, Nisswa. Call 218-963-2620.

**Northland Arboretum,** 14250 Conservation Drive, Brainerd. Call 218-829-8770.

**Pequot Lakes Fire Tower,** CR 11, Pequot Lakes. Call 218-568-5860.

**Pirate's Cove Mini-Golf,** 17992 MN 371 North, Brainerd. Call 218-828-9002. Website: www.piratescove.net.

**Rainy Days,** 25491 Main Street, Nisswa. Call 218-963-4891; 800-635-7809.

**Simpler Thymes of Nisswa,** 25410 Main Street, Nisswa. Call 218-963-9463. Website: www.simplerthymesofnisswa.com

**This Old Farm Pioneer Village and Paul Bunyan Land,** 17553 MN 18, Brainerd. Call 218-764-2524. Website: www.thisoldfarm.net.

**Totem Pole,** 25485 Main Street, Nisswa. Call 218-963-3450; 866-506-5244. Website: www.totempolemn.com.

## Dining

**371 Diner,** 14901 Edgewood Drive, Brainerd. Call 218-829-3356.

**A-Pine Family Restaurant,** 33039 Old MN 371, Pequot Lakes. Call 218-568-8353.

**Adirondack Coffee,** 25503 Main Street, Nisswa. Call 218-967-0111. Website: http://lovemymug.com.

**Black Bear Lodge and Saloon,** 14819 Edgewood Drive, Brainerd. Call 218-828-8400. Website: www.blackbearlodgemn.com.

**Grand Casino Mille Lacs,** 777 Grand Avenue, Onamia. Call 800-626-5825. Website: www.grand casinomn.com.

**Izatys,** 40005 85th Avenue, Onamia. Call 800-533-1728. Website: www .izatys.com.

The 371 Diner in Brainerd.

**Lost Lake Lodge,** 7965 Lost Lake Road, Lake Shore. Call 218-963-2681; 800-450-2681. Website: www.lostlake.com.

**Prairie Bay Grill,** 15115 Edgewood Drive, Baxter. Call 218-824-6444. Website: www.prairiebay.com.

**Sawmill Inn,** 601 Washington Street, Brainerd. Call 218-829-5444.

**Svoboda's Spotlite,** 111 Madison Street, Garrison. Call 320-692-4692.

**The Tiki Room,** Jack Pine Center, Pequot Lakes. Call 218-568-8373.

**Timberjack Smokehouse & Saloon,** 4443 CR 168, Pequot Lakes. Call 218-568-6070. Website: www.timberjacksmokehouse.com.

**Zorbaz on the Lake,** CR 66, Crosslake. Call 218-692-4567. Website: www.zorbaz.com.

## Other Contacts

**Brainerd Lakes Chamber,** 7393 MN 371, Brainerd. Call 218-829-2838; 800-450-2838. Website: www.explorebrainerdlakes.com

**Mille Lacs Lake Area Tourism,** 204 Roosevelt Road, Onamia. Call 320-532-5626; 888-350-2692. Website: www.millelacs.com.

*Statue of author Vilhelm Moberg in Chisago City.*

CHAPTER

9

# St. Croix River Valley and America's Little Sweden

**Estimated length:** 120 miles
**Estimated time:** 4 hours

**Getting there:** From the Twin Cities, take I-35W north to US 8 east to Chisago City. Follow US 8 east through Lindstrom, Center City, and Taylors Falls. Take US 8 south to MN 95 (St. Croix Trail) to reach Franconia. Continue on MN 95 to MN 97, turning right to arrive in Scandia. Return to MN 95 and travel south to County Route (CR 4) (Maple Street) to stop in Marine on St. Croix. Follow MN 95 south to Stillwater. From Stillwater, you can take MN 96 or MN 36 back to the Twin Cities.

**Highlights:** The Scandinavian bakeries in the "America's Little Sweden" towns; the steep bluffs and cliffs of Interstate State Park; the Taylors Falls Angel Hill District; the Gammelgården Museum; the Franconia Sculpture Garden; antiquing and dining in Stillwater.

There are lakes in this area, but the primary source of outdoor recreation in the St. Croix Valley rests along the riverbanks. This small but highly scenic region derives its beauty from the St. Croix River and the surrounding landscapes. The wealthy New England families that settled here more than a century ago re-created their New England villages along the riverside, small towns that remain intact, as charming and historic as they were when they were first built. Along with the New Englanders came the Scandinavians, building tight agricultural and cultural enclaves. Logging and the fur trade drove the growth of the area during the 19th century, and today's visitors can still find remnants of those trades, primarily in place names, but the small towns are quaint and wonderful to wander around, and going up the river can provide insight into some of Minnesota's Scandinavian heritage. The St. Croix Valley is still full of natural beauty, from rivers to woodlands to prairie to glacial trails, and is a park lover's dream region. Some of Minnesota's most beautiful state parks are in this area, running along the river and offering nearly every kind of recreational opportunity, including swimming, canoeing, hiking, camping, horseback riding, cross-country skiing, and snowshoeing. Artists have not been immune to the area's beauty, and the arts community is strong and growing throughout the Valley.

Inland from the river, in an area heavily populated with lakes and farmland, is a part of the state known as **America's Little Sweden.** A series of small towns settled by Swedish (and other Scandinavian) immigrants, America's Little Sweden is a place you can still hear faint traces of Swedish accents and are likely to see store and street signs in both English and Swedish. Most of these communities have active relationships with sister cities in Sweden, and the food and culture still strongly reflect that ancestry.

**Chisago City** was host to novelist Vilhelm Moberg, author of a four-part cycle of books known as the Emigrant series, which he researched in Chisago City. Today he is remembered by a statue in a park bearing his name. The town's name itself comes from the Native American phrase *ki chi saga,* which means "fair and lovely waters." It's an aptly named community, surrounded by lakes that have made it an enduring tourist destination. You can find a good meal at **Meredee's Bistro,** or wander over to **George's Smokin' BBQ.** Just east of Chisago City is **WineHaven Winery and Vineyard**, an award-winning vineyard that's been family owned and operated for four generations. Take US 8 to CR 80, then the first left onto 292nd Street to find the winery and its tasting room.

Nearby is the town of **Lindstrom,** home to the **Chisago County History Center.** The Emigrant novels by Vilhelm Moberg feature a fictional couple named Karl Oskar and Kristina. Lindstrom has a statue of the literary couple—along with a water tower shaped like a Swedish coffeepot. From Lindstrom, travel south on CR 25, then east on Glader Boulevard to reach **Kichi-Saga Park,** home to **Nya Duvemåla.** This old house was an inspiration to Moberg, who modeled Karl Oskar and Kristina's fictional home after it. A boulder in front of the house was donated by Volvo from Åseda, Sweden. Stop for a bite to eat at the **Swedish Inn,** especially the Swedish pancakes, or go more American at **Dinnerbel.** Or even better, visit the **Lindstrom Bakery** for both Swedish and non-Swedish baked goods, many organic.

**Center City** has the distinction of being the oldest continuously settled Swedish community in Minnesota, having been founded in 1851. (In a non-Swedish-related note, it's also home to the internationally renowned Hazelden Center for addiction treatment.) Center City is on the shores of Kichi-Saga, or "the Big Lake." It's also known as Swede Lake, and it used to be one enormous connected lake until the expansion of the railroads caused it to be broken into five separate lakes. Center City is home to **Chisago Lake Evangelical Lutheran Church,** which has operated continuously since 1854 and has been in its current building since 1889. Original homes of the Swedish pioneers can be seen at the **Center City Historic District** on Summit Avenue, which has numerous houses of first- and second-generation families, built in period style.

Just outside Center City on US 8 is **Eichten's Bistro & Market,** a restaurant and food shop filled with bison and artisan cheeses produced locally by Eichten's Hidden Acres farm. Try a bison burger, especially the Blue Mox with Minnesota cave-aged blue cheese, and pick up some cheese and sausage for the road.

Continuing on US 8 will bring you to **Taylors Falls.** It's hard to imagine a more dramatic entrance, as the road suddenly curves, opening up soaring views of the **St. Croix Dalles,** a deep canyon gouged out during the last ice age. The St. Croix River has steep bluffs on both sides, with forests of pine, oak, and maple trees lining them.

Incorporated in 1858, Taylors Falls has retained its small-town sensibilities as well its old sense of history. **Folsom House** looks like it was plucked out of a New England landscape, along with several neighbors, and replanted in Taylors Falls. Home of a lumber baron and state senator, the Folsom House is a study in life 150 years ago. The home was owned by five generations of Folsoms, and family members tended to store furnishings and belongings rather than divest them, so the museum is a treasure trove of authentic pieces, including kitchenware, clothing (even a Civil War uniform), and furniture. After visiting the Folsom House, take some time to explore (by foot or by car) the homes on the hills above the museum, known collectively as the **Angel Hill District.**

*Eichten's Bistro & Market, Center City.*

There are historic lodging options in Taylors Falls. **The Old Jail** has three suites and a cottage in two buildings, one a former jail, the other having housed a wide variety of businesses: saloon, chicken-plucking factory, and mortuary. Despite its gruesome history, the suites are lovely, all including private bath, some including old-fashioned record players, one including a bathroom in a cave, and one not recommended for people over 6 feet tall. The **Cottage** has only one unit, but it's a suite with private dining area overlooking the St. Croix River in an 18th-century house.

When it's time for dinner, check out Tangled Up in Blue, a French fusion restaurant, with upscale fare and a good wine list. If you're looking for something more casual (and you're visiting in the summer), stop by The Drive In. It's retro, it's got a giant rotating root beer cup on a stick, and burgers and malts are served to your vehicle by carhops. Bonus: it's right next door to a mini-golf course. Other good choices are Smitty's Border Bar & Grill and Schoony's Malt Shop & Pizzeria.

The biggest draw of the Taylors Falls area is outdoor recreation. The headquarters for information is the St. Croix Visitor Center, in St. Croix Falls, Wisconsin, which is just across the river from Taylors Falls. As the St. Croix ambles south along the Minnesota border, canoeing and camping are popular activities, but check with the visitors center before making plans—there are restrictions regarding use of campsites and boats to protect the river itself and the land on either side of it. In times of low rainfall, fire restrictions are strictly enforced.

Take US 8 to the only stoplight and turn left, then follow CR 16 to Wild Mountain. Wild Mountain takes advantage of the rolling terrain in the river area to run 25 ski and boarding runs during the winter, along with a snow-tubing course. During the summer, there's a water park with alpine slide and go-cart tracks, as well as public and private charter river cruises, canoe and kayak rental, and an RV park and campground.

The dramatic terrain plays a role in several state parks in the area. North of Taylors Falls on MN 95, turn onto CR 12 to find **Wild River State Park.** This sizable park along 18 miles of the St. Croix River offers hiking and cross-country ski trails, and a guesthouse and camping within the park, including campsites for visitors with horses. Spring provides some of the most beautiful wildflower displays in the state. For those with GPS units and an itch to explore, the Minnesota DNR website provides coordinates for historical searches within the park. If you'd like to find lodging nearby, check out the **Women's Environmental Institute at Amador Hill.** Located in an organic apple orchard on the edge of Wild River State Park, the WEI offers four rooms for guests or groups. Two of the rooms share a bath, and the largest room has a fireplace. The rooms are simple but attractive; it's the location that makes this a worthwhile getaway.

At the junction of US 8 and MN 95 is the **Franconia Sculpture Park.** The park is, intentionally, a work in progress. There are more than 75 exhibits in this rural exhibition area, and each year somewhere between 15 and 25 artists are invited to work and contribute art on a rotating basis. The artworks are spread across a field with flat mowed paths; self-guided tours and guided tours are offered. Not only are many of the pieces in process, but several are hands-on for visitors—very attractive for kids.

Travel south on MN 95 to MN 97, which will bring you to **Scandia,** the first Swedish settlement in Minnesota. Scandia's heritage is displayed

## GLACIAL POTHOLES?

**Interstate State Park** is located on US 8 just as you arrive in Taylors Falls. The park's name reflects its cross-river location, with the park stretching from Minnesota to Wisconsin. River access makes kayaking and canoeing popular, and interesting geological formations, including exposed lava flows and glacial deposits, make this an intriguing area for exploration. Of particular interest are the glacial potholes, immense holes (the deepest one is 60 feet) in the bedrock where the Glacial St. Croix River forced its way through. Interstate State Park has more of these glacial potholes in one area than any other place in the world. Rock climbing is popular, and during the fall, the autumn colors provide a major draw.

at **Gammelgården,** a living history museum paying tribute to the Scandinavian roots of the region. Several original immigrant homes and other buildings, including a church, have been restored on 11 acres of farmland.

*Hay Lake School, Scandia.*

The site is open for public tours during the summer, but year-round the museum offers a vast array of special events and classes, including music festivals, sausage-making classes, and annual Midsommar Dag (Midsummer Day) and Lucia Day celebrations.

If Gammelgården isn't enough history for you, check out the nearby **Hay Lake School Museum,** a mile south of Scandia on CR 3. Listed on the National Register of Historic Places, this museum is made up of a former schoolhouse and a log home built in the late 1800s.

You can get breakfast or lunch at the **Scandia Café,** just down the street from Gammelgården. It's a classic small-town café, often busy with locals who come in for the daily soup specials and turkey luncheon.

From Scandia, return to US 95 and drive south to **William O'Brien State Park.** This small but lovely park was named after a lumber baron who had originally cleared the land of trees. The park is now (more than a century later) reforested and full of wildlife and river access. It's open year-round and offers trails for cross-country skiing and snowshoeing, as well as campsites with electricity for winter camping. There's a swimming beach in the summer with a large picnic area adjacent, and canoeing on the river is made possible by rentals in the park. Canoe shuttle service is offered during summer. Birdwatchers can spot hundreds of different birds. The visitors center has a seasonal checklist of what might be seen, from the more commonly found Canadian goose and northern flicker to the uncommon (but still possible!) great blue heron, ruffed grouse, and scarlet tanager.

Just 2 miles south of William O'Brien State Park on MN 95 is **Marine on St. Croix,** a tiny riverside village. The town was originally founded as a sawmill, the **Marine Mill,** the first commercial sawmill on the St. Croix River. Today the Marine Mill is gone, but its site is maintained as in interpretive site by the Minnesota Historical Society. You can wander down trails with signs that explain the significance of the site and include photos of what once existed. The trail takes you to an overlook above the river.

You can see more of the village's history at the **Stone House Museum.** Aptly named for its Scandinavian stone architecture, the Stone House Museum was originally the town meetinghouse. Today it's a repository for artifacts and photographs documenting the Scandinavian settlers in the early 19th century.

You can grab a bite to eat for breakfast or lunch at **Roberta's of Marine,** a coffee shop with organic coffees, tasty pastries, and delicious soups. Or you can pick up snacks to go (among many other things) at the **Marine General Store.** If you'd like to stay a bit longer, book a room at the **Asa Parker House.** This lovely Greek Revival home, built in 1856, overlooks the village of Marine on St. Croix. There are four guest rooms, all with private bath; the Alice O'Brien suite (named after the O'Brien lumber family daughter who donated land for the William O'Brien State Park, above) has a private porch. The property is close enough to Stillwater for easy access to restaurants and shops, but just far enough to provide an idyllic, peaceful retreat.

**Stillwater,** south of Marine on St. Croix, calls itself the "Birthplace of Minnesota." Built by lumber barons and transplanted New Englanders, it's one of the oldest cities in the state. Like any town that suffers the loss of its primary industry, Stillwater went through its slump in the early 20th century. But the natural beauty surrounding the area combined with the charm of the downtown streets and buildings drove a renaissance that has created thriving shops and galleries and a busy tourist trade, particularly on summer weekends, when driving down Main Street can require patience and time.

But the payoff is in the ability to stop, shop, wander along the river and watch the Stillwater Lift Bridge operate, see the sailboats and yachts dotting the water, and have almost more choices of places to dine than seems reasonable. Whether you are wandering on your own for a private retreat, as part of a couples romantic getaway, or with a family, Stillwater

*Stillwater's Lift Bridge.*

## HOT-AIR BALLOON RIDES

Given the beautiful scenery and the charming small towns, it's only logical that hot-air balloon rides would be a popular pastime. The following companies all offer hot-air balloon service daily from May through October, weather permitting. Contact the individual companies for off-season possibilities (contact information is at the end of this chapter).

**Stillwater Balloons:** Morning or late afternoon departures are offered during the summer, but balloon rides (dependent on weather) can be done all year long, and all flights conclude with a champagne celebration. **Wiederkehr Balloons:** Morning and afternoon departures are available, with up to eight passengers booked for a 12-passenger balloon. Champagne is served at the conclusion of the ride. **Aamodt's Hot Air Balloon Rides:** Hot-air balloon rides are offered with departures from the owner's apple orchard in Stillwater. Rides are reserved for two people only and include a champagne toast. Most rides are scheduled late in the day to take advantage of the views over the St. Croix, but sunrise departures can be accommodated.

is a lovely place to spend a day or two. Add in the recreation and dining options south of Stillwater, and the stay could be longer.

Of course there's history to be found. The **Warden's House** was built in 1853 and used as a residence for prison wardens and superintendents until 1941, when the building was sold to the Washington County Historical Society. Several of the rooms are furnished as they would have been in the late 19th century, while a few rooms are reserved for displays relevant to the region's overall history, including the lumber industry and children's items. The **Joseph Wolf Caves** were once used for breweries, and today tours illuminate both the caves and the history behind the brewing.

Options for exploring the river town abound, by land and by sea. The **St. Croix Boat & Packet Company** offers cruises on the St. Croix River with your choice of a lunch, dinner, brunch, or live music cruises. Boats are also available for private charter. Reservations are recommended. For something more personal, try **Gondola Romantica.** Who needs Venice? This company brings romantic gondola rides right onto the St. Croix River. Options include everything from 20-minute sightseeing cruises to a five-course dinner cruise. The company offers customized cruises as well. Gondolas hold six people, but if you'd like a private excursion, reserve ahead.

The **Stillwater Trolley** operates enclosed, climate-controlled trolleys that take visitors on a 45-minute guided tour of the Stillwater area.

If you really want to experience the history of Stillwater in a hands-on way, **Lumberjack Sports Camps** are your best bet. Taking place each year during Lumberjack Days, they will put you to work learning about log rolling and cross-cut sawing.

One of the joys of Stillwater is the abundance of historic (and romantic) inns and bed & breakfasts. It's a treat to spend a weekend in this river town—and it's also popular. Book ahead.

The **Lowell Inn** is the granddaddy of historic hotels in Stillwater. Built in 1927 on the site of a former lumberjack hotel, this stately building has 23 impeccably decorated rooms, some with stained-glass windows, antique furnishings, and fireplaces, but all with modern conveniences. Several

---

## BED & BREAKFASTS

The **Elephant Walk** is an elaborate Victorian house, the residence of globe-trotting owners who have filled the interior with finds from their travels in Europe and Asia. Each of the four sumptuously decorated rooms has a theme: the Rangoon, Chiang Mai, Cadiz, and Raffles rooms are all decorated according to their geographic designation. All rooms have fireplaces and refrigerators with complimentary nonalcoholic beverages; a bottle of wine and appetizers, as well as a four-course breakfast, are included in the rates.

The whimsical **Ann Bean Mansion** has a colorful history, complete with riches and scandal, and today it has five lovely rooms, all with fireplaces and private baths. The Tower Room is a particularly cozy choice. Rooms come with plush robes, and rates include an afternoon glass of wine and full breakfast daily.

Sitting on a hillside above Stillwater, the **Rivertown Inn** provides beautiful views along with four rooms and five suites, all elaborately decorated and named after literary heavyweights (Lord Byron, Longfellow). The inn is open year-round, but summer visitors will enjoy the use of the private gardens and screened gazebo. All accommodations have luxurious bedding, plush robes, turn-down service with handmade chocolates, full breakfast, and evening social hour.

The lovingly restored 1895 Queen Anne home **Lady Goodwood** has several original details, include a parlor fireplace. The three guest rooms are all lavishly decorated in Victorian style and have private baths; the St. Croix Suite comes with a round king-sized bed.

rooms have Jacuzzis. The romance factor here is high. The hotel also has a highly regarded restaurant.

The **Water Street Inn** is a small luxury inn with rooms and suites, most with gas fireplaces. The rooms are decorated as would have befitted the upscale visitors of the lumber boom days, and several packages are offered involving meals, flowers, and massages. A well-regarded restaurant and pub round out the amenities.

The lower St. Croix Valley enjoys an affluent resident population and close proximity to the Twin Cities, giving it an abundance of notable dining options, even off-season. **Luna Rossa** bills itself as an Italian steakhouse, but that's somewhat of a misnomer; there are plenty of steak and grilled meat options, but the restaurant also has a respectable list of Italian pasta and pizza dishes that are equally worthy of attention. The menu changes seasonally at **Savories,** a European bistro-themed restaurant, and there is always something innovative offered. Entrées combine Italian with Latin foods, and vegetarians are not ignored. Don't skip dessert.

It's open year-round, but the **Dock Café** is the place to be during the warm-weather months. Situated right on the banks of the St. Croix, the Dock Café has outdoor seating that gives diners a full view of river life. Not surprisingly, the outdoor patio is popular—plan to arrive early, or wait. However, the indoor ambience is attractive as well, with a fireplace and wide windows. Menu items run heavily to meats and seafood.

**Aprille's Showers Tea Room** is exactly what it says: a traditional tearoom. Walk-ins welcome, but call ahead for special theme teas, including American Girl doll tea parties.

Within the historic **Lowell Inn** are two restaurants worth noting. The formal restaurant, in the elegant **George Washington Room,** serves classic formal dinner foods such as duck à l'orange and beef Wellington, while the **Matterhorn Room** serves a four-course Swiss dinner fondue each evening.

Tim McKee, a James Beard award winner, created **Smalley's Caribbean Barbeque,** a casual but terrific barbeque joint. It's not just for carnivores—the side dishes are worthy all by themselves.

Stillwater's main city center, along the riverfront, has developed into a visitor's shopping haven, full of small, charming shops, with hardly a chain store to be seen. Antique enthusiasts flock to this community for its large concentration of antique stores and dealers, but there are plenty of other kinds of retail as well.

**North Main Studio** is open only by appointment, but it's worth planning ahead to see where local resident and artist Carl Erickson displays, sells, and creates his pottery. **Tamarack Gallery** showcases local and national artists, who are represented in various mediums, including painting, etching, sculpture, and photography.

**Northern Vineyards** is an award-winning winery right on the main street of Stillwater, using Minnesota and Wisconsin grapes. It's open daily for tastings and tours. In the summer, enjoy a glass of wine on their back patio, overlooking the lift bridge across the river.

**Loome Antiquarian Booksellers** is the bookseller for serious book collectors, with hundreds of thousands of books available. There are also framed engravings for sale, as well as medieval manuscript leaves. A short walk away is the shop's sister store, **Loome Theological Booksellers,** specializing in secondhand books on theology and religion.

Located in an historic mill, the **Mill Antiques** is comprised of nearly 80 antique and collectibles dealers spread over three floors. A great spot for serious antiquing or window shopping. Another good source for antique enthusiasts, the **Midtown Antique Mall** has more than one hundred dealers, including several furniture dealers.

To reach the final stop on this route, take MN 95 south to **Afton,** the home of two notable outdoor areas:

**Afton Alps** is one of the biggest Minnesota ski resorts, with 40 trails and 18 lifts, a snowboard park and tubing hill. During the summer, the resort is open for mountain bikers, and an 18-hole course is available for golfers.

**Afton State Park** is a beautiful nature preserve that provides a strenuous workout for visitors. There are 20 miles of hiking trails, most of which have some sharply steep inclines. However, the views of the St. Croix River make it worth the effort. One area allows horseback riders, and several miles of trail are open for cross-country skiers in the winter. Year-round camping is available.

If you'd like to linger at this end of the trail, reserve a room at the **Afton House Inn.** Afton House has 46 rooms, most with canopy or four-poster bed, and deluxe rooms have balconies overlooking the St. Croix River. The location near Afton Alps makes this a good choice for a ski weekend with a warm, romantic hideaway to return to at the end of the day. The inn has a restaurant and bar on-site.

# IN THE AREA

## Accommodations

**Afton House Inn,** 3291 South St. Croix Trail, Afton. Call 651-436-8883. Website: www.aftonhouseinn.com.

**The Ann Bean Mansion,** 319 West Pine Street, Stillwater. Call 651-430-0355; 877-837-4400. Website: www.annbeanmansion.com.

**Asa Parker House,** 17500 St. Croix Trail North, Marine on St. Croix. Call 651-433-5248; 888-857-9969. Website: www.asaparkerbb.com.

**The Cottage,** 950 Fox Glen Drive, Taylors Falls. Call 651-465-3595. Website: www.the-cottage.com.

**The Elephant Walk,** 801 West Pine Street, Stillwater. Call 651-430-0528; 888-430-0359. Website: www.elephantwalkbb.com.

**Lady Goodwood,** 704 First Street South, Stillwater. Call 651-439-3771; 866-688-5239. Website: www.ladygoodwood.com.

**Lowell Inn,** 102 North Second Street, Stillwater. Call 651 439-1100. Website: www.lowellinn.com.

**The Old Jail,** 349 Government Street, Taylors Falls. Call 651-465-3112. Website: www.oldjail.com.

**Rivertown Inn,** 306 West Olive Street, Stillwater. Call 651-430-2955. Website: www.rivertowninn.com.

**Water Street Inn,** 101 Water Street South. Call 651-439-6000. Website: www.waterstreetinn.us.

**Women's Environmental Institute at Amador Hill,** 15715 River Road, North Branch. Call 651-583-0705. Website: www.w-e-i.org.

## Attractions and Recreation

**Aamodt's Hot Air Balloon Rides,** Stillwater. Call 651-351-0101; 866-546-8247. Website: www.aamodtsballoons.com.

**Afton Alps,** Afton. Call 651-436-5245; 800-328-1328. Website: www .aftonalps.com.

**Afton State Park,** Afton. Call 651-436-5391. Website: www.dnr.state.mn .us/state_parks/afton/index.html.

**Chisago County History Center,** 13112 Third Avenue North, Lindstrom. Call: 651-257-5310. Website: www.chisagocountyhistory.org.

**Chisago Lake Evangelical Lutheran Church,** Center City. Call 651-257-6300. Website: www.chisagolakelutheranchurch.org.

**Folsom House,** 272 West Government Street, Taylors Falls. Call 651-465-3125. Website: www.mnhs.org/places/sites/fh/.

*The Folsom House, Taylors Falls.*

**Franconia Sculpture Park,** US 8 and MN 95, Franconia. Call 651-257-6668. Website: www.franconia.org.

**Gammelgården,** 20880 Olinda Trail, Scandia. Call 651-433-5053. Website: www.gammelgardenmuseum.org.

**Gondola Romantica,** 425 East Nelson Street, Stillwater. Call 651-439-1783. Website: www.gondolaromantica.com.

**Hay Lake School Museum,** Olinda Trail North and Old Marine Trail, Scandia. Call 651-433-4014. Website: http://wchsmn.org/museums/scandia/.

**Interstate State Park,** US 8, Taylors Falls. Call 651-465-5711. Website: www.dnr.state.mn.us/state_parks/interstate/index.html.

**Joseph Wolf Caves,** 420 South Main Street, Stillwater. Call 651-292-1220.

**Loome Antiquarian/Theological Booksellers,** 320 North Fourth Street, Stillwater. Call 651-430-1092. Website: www.loomebooks.com.

**Lumberjack Sports Camps,** 12360 75th Street, Stillwater. Call 651-439-5626.

**Midtown Antique Mall,** 301 South Main Street, Stillwater. Call 651-430-0808. Website: www.midtownantiques.com.

**The Mill Antiques,** 410 North Main Street, Stillwater. Call 651-430-1816.

**North Main Studio,** 402 North Main Street, Stillwater. Call 651-351-1379. Website: www.northmainstudio.com.

**Northern Vineyards,** 223 North Main Street, Stillwater. Call 651-430-1032. Website: www.northernvineyards.com.

**Nya Duvemåla,** CR 25 and Glader Boulevard, Lindstrom.

**St. Croix Boat & Packet Company,** 525 South Main Street, Stillwater. Call 651-430-1234. Website: www.andiamo-ent.com.

**Stillwater Balloons,** 14791 North 60th Street, Stillwater. Call 651-439-1800. Website: www.stillwaterballoons.com.

**Stillwater Trolley,** 400 East Nelson Street, Stillwater. Call 651-430-0352. Website: www.stillwatertrolley.com.

**Stone House Museum,** 241 Fifth Street, Marine on St. Croix. Call 651-433-2061.

**Tamarack Gallery,** 112 South Main Street, Stillwater. Call 651-439-9393. Website: www.tamarackgallery.com.

**Warden's House Museum,** 602 North Main Street, Stillwater. Call 651-439-5956. Website: http://wchsmn.org/museums/wardens_house.

**Wiederkehr Balloons,** Lakeland. Call 651-436-8172.

**Wild Mountain & Taylors Falls Recreation,** 37200 Wild Mountain Road, Taylors Falls. Call 651-465-6315; 800-447-4958. Website: www.wild mountain.com.

**Wild River State Park,** 39797 Park Trail, Center City. Call 651-583-2125. Website: www.dnr.state.mn.us/state_parks/wild_river/index.html.

**William O'Brien State Park,** 16821 O'Brien Trail North, Marine on St. Croix. Call 651-433-0500. Website: www.dnr.state.mn.us/state_parks/ william_obrien/index.html.

**WineHaven Winery and Vineyard,** 9757 292nd Street, Chisago City. Call 651-257-1017. Website: www.winehaven.com.

## Dining

**Aprille's Showers Tea Room,** 120 North Main Street, Stillwater. Call 651-430-2004. Website: www.aprilleshowers.com.

**Dinnerbel,** 12565 Lake Boulevard, Lindstrom. Call 651-257-9524. Website: www.dinnerbel.com.

**Dock Café,** 425 South Nelson Street, Stillwater. Call 651-430-3770. Website: www.dockcafe.com.

**The Drive In,** 572 Bench Street, Taylors Falls. Call 651-465-7831. Website: www.taylorsfalls.com.

*Wild River State Park.*

**Eichten's Bistro & Market,** 16440 Lake Boulevard, Center City. Call 651-257-1566. Website: www.theeichtensbistro.com.

**George's Smokin' BBQ,** 29346 Old Towne Road, Chisago City. Call 651-257-3227.

**Lindstrom Bakery,** 12830 Lake Boulevard, Lindstrom. Call 651-257-1374.

**Lowell Inn,** 102 North Second Street, Stillwater. Call 651-439-1100. Website: www.lowellinn.com.

**Luna Rossa,** 402 South Main Street, Stillwater. Call 651-430-0560. Website: www.lunarossawinebar.com.

**Meredee's Bistro,** 11347 North Avenue, Chisago City. Call 651-257-9144. Website: www.meredeesbistro.com.

**Roberta's of Marine,** 41 Judd Street, Marine on St. Croix. Call 651-433-9926.

**Savories,** 108 North Main Street, Stillwater. Call 651-430-0702. Website: www.savoriesbistro.com.

**Scandia Café,** 21079 Olinda Trail North, Scandia. Call 651-433-4054. Website: www.scandiamn.com/scandiacafe/index.htm.

**Schoony's Malt Shop & Pizzeria,** 384 Bench Street, Taylors Falls. Call 651-465-3222.

**Smalley's Caribbean Barbeque,** 423 Main Street South, Stillwater. Call 651-439-5375.

**Smitty's Border Bar & Grill,** 367 Bench Street, Taylors Falls. Call 651-465-1011.

**Swedish Inn,** 12678 Lake Boulevard, Lindstrom. Call 651-257-4072.

**Tangled Up in Blue,** 425 Bench Street, Taylors Falls. Call 651-465-1000.

## Other Contacts

**Falls Chamber of Commerce,** St. Croix Falls. Call 715-483-3850.

**Greater Stillwater Chamber of Commerce,** 1950 Northwestern Avenue, Suite 101, Stillwater. Call 651-439-4001. Website: www.ilovestillwater.com.

**Swedish Circle Tours.** Website: www.swedishcircletours.com.

*Frontenac State Park.*

CHAPTER

10

# Northern Mississippi River Bluff Country:
## Hastings to Lake City

**Estimated length:** 65 miles
**Estimated time:** 2 hours

**Getting there:** From the Twin Cities, take I-494 to MN 55, then take MN 56 to MN 61. Follow MN 61 to Frontenac.

**Highlights:** New England-style architecture and historic sites of Hastings and Red Wing; antique shopping and dining in those towns and Lake City; the stopped-in-time village of Old Frontenac; views of the Mississippi and Lake Pepin. Note: you could combine this with the La Crescent to Wabasha trip (Chapter 11) for a longer journey.

Geological history indicates that the area was sculpted by volcanoes and ancient seas, and more recently by glaciers that carved out some of the region's many rivers. This part of the state features not just one river, although the Mississippi is the major river in the area. The starting point for this trip, **Hastings,** is the point where the St. Croix, Mississippi, and Vermillion rivers converge, and the Cannon River flows into **Red Wing,** where it joins the Mississippi, all results of glaciers ten thousand years ago. As with so many of the other river towns, this area's proximity to the all-important transportation modes that made up early travel boded well for their creation and expansion. Milling and lumber operations were critical to the growth and stability of these towns, but the natural beauty of the region has seen a rise in tourist income as well. Today the rivers are a major source of recreation and sightseeing.

The first stop on this itinerary is the town of Hastings, whose city center has 63 buildings on the National Register of Historic Places. In the town itself is the **LeDuc House,** built in 1866 by Andrew Jackson Downing, a rare historic building that is virtually untouched. The former home of William LeDuc, a commissioner of agriculture under President Rutherford Hayes and a Civil War hero, the building itself is a delight to visit, but the 4.5-acre grounds are lovely to visit as well, encompassing an apple orchard and forests.

Also within the city is the **Vermillion Falls Park,** an oasis with beautiful waterfalls and trails for hiking and biking, and the Vermillion River itself is popular with white-water rafters, although it's a fairly short route. If you're feeling more ambitious, try the **Hastings Trail System,** which has a jumping-on point at Vermillion Falls Park, then circles the city in a 15-mile loop. Scenic viewpoints include the Vermillion River, Mississippi River, Lake Isabel, and Lake Rebecca.

To visit the **Carpenter St. Croix Valley Nature Center,** take MN 61 north from Hastings to MN 10; travel east on MN 10 to County Route 21 (CR 21) and travel north. This small (425 acres) but lavish nature preserve was once a private estate and apple orchard. Today it is a well-maintained

---

### HISTORIC DOWNTOWN HASTINGS

Built during the heyday of river travel, and for a long time the last port reachable year-round on the Mississippi, Hastings still has a strong Victorian sensibility in its buildings, with 63 listed on the National Register of Historic Places. The downtown itself is a National Register Historic District, known officially as the **East Second Street Commercial Historic District.** Thirty-five buildings constructed before 1900 have retained their beautiful Victorian detailing and Old World charm. A map of the district is available from the Chamber of Commerce or city hall.

In addition to the commercial district, there is also the **Hastings Second Street Residential District,** comprised of homes built prior to 1890. The architecture of these homes includes Italianate, Greek Revival, and French Second Empire.

natural area, the release site for the University of Minnesota's Raptor Reha-
bilitation Program, and offers 10 miles of trails, some of which have been
adapted for visitors with limited mobility.

To fully experience the historic river-town atmosphere, consider booking a room at the **Classic Rosewood Inn**. This beautiful 1880 Queen Anne
house has been updated to include modern amenities in a classic B&B
venue. Eight rooms and suites, all with private bath and some with fireplaces and whirlpools, are richly decorated and large enough to allow massage therapists to set up tables for private sessions (reserve in advance). A
full breakfast is included each day, either in the dining room or privately.

When it's time for a meal, stop by the **Levee Café**. The Levee Café is a
nice friendly restaurant where kids are welcome and is open most days for
lunch and dinner. Specialties are pasta and seafood.

If you're looking for a more grown-up dinner, **Current on the Mississippi** is an upscale-appearing but reasonably priced restaurant serving Italian specialties as well as steakhouse fare.

Like most of the historic river towns, Hastings has no shortage of shopping opportunities, especially of the antique variety. The streets around the
Current on the Mississippi have several good antiques shops, including **The
Emporium**, a two-story antiques and consignment gallery specializing in
vintage furniture, dolls, jewelry, and primitive tools and pottery. **Antiques
on Main** has 20 dealers, many of whom buy entire estates. **The Briar Patch**
specializes in clothing, jewelry, and accessories.

Not all the shopping is about antiques, though. **Scandinavian Marketplace** has an extensive collection of Scandinavian home and gift items,
including hand-painted furniture, tableware, clothing, books, music, and
toys. **Mississippi Clayworks** offers locally made pottery, including custom
orders.

If you're in the mood for a little gambling side trip, take MN 316 from
Hastings south to 200th Street, then follow 200th for 8 miles to find the
**Treasure Island Resort and Casino** in Welch. Slots, blackjack, poker, and
bingo are all available in this massive complex as well as four restaurants
and several cocktail bars and an attached hotel and marina. The hotel has
an elaborate indoor pool, fitness center, and child-care center.

Coming south out of Hastings, follow MN 61 to CR 7, or Welch Village
Road, to spend some quality winter time on the slopes of **Welch Village**.
Welch has fifty runs of varying difficulty for skiers and snowboarders as
well as a terrain park. The Village also offers slopeside bunkhouses for

## ALEXIS BAILLY VINEYARD

Head south on MN 61 from Hastings and follow the signs at 170th Street to visit the **Alexis Bailly Vineyard.** Yes, you can grow grapes in Minnesota—it just takes tenacity. Alexis Bailly is Minnesota's first and arguably foremost vineyard. David Bailly planted his first crop of grapes in 1973, against the advice of viticulturists who warned that no grapes could survive a Minnesota winter. Yet by 1978, Bailly produced his first vintage. The winery works with classic and newbreed grapes that have been found to withstand extreme cold. In fact, their motto is "Where the grapes can suffer." Apparently suffering works, because Alexis Bailly has won national awards for its wines. Today Bailly's daughter Nan is the winemaker and runs the vineyard, and has an expansive line of wines, including the ice wine Isis; Voyageur, a blend of French and grapes developed at the University of Minnesota to withstand winter; and Ratafia, an orange-infused dessert wine. The vineyard is open seasonally for tours and tastings and offers numerous special events, including chocolate and cheese tastings and jazz nights. Bring a picnic to enjoy on the grounds, but no need to carry along the bocce balls—the bocce courts on-site are supplied.

rental, which are rustic with shared baths but offer the utmost in convenient access for devoted skiers and boarders. You can also rent tubes and canoes in Welch to take out on the Cannon River, as well as arrange for canoe shuttle services.

The town of Welch is also a connecting point for the **Cannon Valley Trail,** a 20-mile paved trail that runs on an old railroad track from Cannon Falls to Red Wing along the Cannon River. The trail winds through shifting terrain that is home to a diverse collection of flora and fauna, including the Minnesota dwarf trout lily, wild turkeys, osprey, pileated woodpeckers, and even an occasional moose or, even more rarely, a wood turtle.

Return to MN 61 and travel south to visit Red Wing, which offers boundless opportunities to explore the world outdoors. The drive itself, which veers east to run along the Mississippi River, is part of the **Great River Road,** a scenic byway that runs from Canada to the Gulf of Mexico. From Red Wing, the Great River Road travels via MN 61 to La Crescent, showcasing 107 miles of river views, forests, small historic river towns and villages, and countless opportunities for natural and wildlife exploration.

*City park in Red Wing.*

In Red Wing itself, learn about local history at the **Goodhue County Historical Society.** This sizable regional museum has extensive collections on numerous aspects of the area's history, including archaeology, business, geology, immigration, and agriculture. A clothing exhibit has samples for kids to try out, and there's a tepee to play in. Note: the society is also in the process of placing signage throughout the county, noting the prior existence of what are now known as ghost towns.

There's another type of history museum near the river at the **Red Wing Shoe Museum.** Red Wing Shoes are indeed manufactured in Red Wing, and this small but lively museum in the Riverfront Centre has hands-on and historical exhibits showing how the shoes are made and sold, including the opportunity to try to build your own shoe.

Another famous local manufacturer has its own museum: the **Red Wing Pottery Museum,** located within the **Pottery Place Historic Center.** Just like the shoes, Red Wing Pottery is made in Red Wing, and it has a museum with displays illustrating the pottery process and history, and an impressive collection of finished objects and historical pieces. The Pottery Place Historic Center itself is worth a visit. Not all shopping malls are bland boxes. The Pottery Place Mall, in a renovated pottery factory, houses a variety of specialty retailers, including art galleries and stores selling antiques, home furnishings, gifts, and fine chocolates.

The **Sheldon Theatre** is named after businessman and former city council member Theodore Sheldon, who donated money to the city to be used in a beneficial but nonsectarian manner. The theater opened in 1904 as an elaborate "jewel box" of a building, full of ornate flourishes in honor of its prominent resident namesake. However, during the Depression, the building was renovated into a movie theater, and much of its architectural grandeur was downscaled. It wasn't until the mid-1980s that the city, with strong support from its residents, decided to restore the Sheldon to its former glory. Today it's host to a wide variety of local, regional, and national arts groups, everything from serious theater to dance to musicals.

There's almost an overabundance of great lodging choices in and around Red Wing. Note: this is a popular weekend getaway destination, so book ahead. The **St. James Hotel** was built in 1875 and has rooms with a handsome Victorian decor; larger rooms have whirlpools, and two deluxe rooms include spacious seating areas. **Moondance Inn** is a beautiful stone inn with five spacious guest rooms, all with private bath and fireplaces, featuring antique furniture and sumptuous decorations. Right next to the Moondance is the **Guesthouse Next Door**, a 1904 Victorian home that is rented as a whole unit. It holds 10 people, and children and pets are welcome. The **Candlelight Inn** is a striking Victorian house offering five rooms and suites, all with private baths and fireplaces. While all the rooms are beautifully decorated, the Butternut Suite in particular is a lesson in opulence and luxury. Full breakfast and afternoon appetizers, wine, and lemonade provided for guests daily. The **Golden Lantern Inn** was built in 1923 by the former president of the Red Wing Shoe Company. This English Tudor has five lush rooms and suites and several public rooms available to guests. Bedrooms all have private baths, and some have fireplaces, sitting rooms, and private balconies. Full breakfast is included daily and is available in the dining room, bedroom, or (during warmer months) on the stone patio. During the summer months, guests have access to the lavish gardens behind the inn. Take MN 61 four miles south of Red Wing to Wildwood Lane to find **Round Barn Farm,** built in 1861. Round Barn offers five spacious rooms beautifully decorated in vintage country style, complete with antique furniture, private baths, and fireplaces or Franklin stoves. Breakfast is provided daily in the dining room, which features a massive limestone fireplace. The property is located on 35 acres complete with walking trails and a gazebo.

Red Wing provides a similarly large number of dining options. The **Port Restaurant** is located in the St. James Hotel. This warmly elegant romantic restaurant offers steakhouse foods (steaks, seafood, pasta) with unconventional twists. The food is excellent, and reservations are strongly recommended. Also located at the St. James Hotel is the **Veranda,** open daily for breakfast and lunch. A more casual full-service restaurant, the Veranda overlooks the Mississippi with outdoor dining in-season. **Liberty's** is open daily for all three meals. There can be no complaints about access to this restaurant—not only do they deliver throughout Red Wing, they also provide free shuttle service to and from boats and hotels. The menu aims to please with Italian, Mexican, burgers, and steaks; breakfast includes all-you-can-eat pancakes. **Oar d'oeuvre** is a nautically themed restaurant and full bar offering a menu that changes seasonally, with an emphasis on hors d'oeuvres and lighter fare. **Lily's Coffee House & Flowers** is the quintessential charming small-town coffee shop and café, with a surprisingly sizable menu includes sandwiches, salads, and soups, plus a wide variety of coffee drinks.

The small town of **Frontenac** is a few miles south of Red Wing on MN 61, and nearby is **Old Frontenac.** The railroads brought people to the community, and they stayed for the scenery. Some of the wealthier visitors built summer homes along Lake Pepin (a naturally occurring lake in the Mississippi River), in what is now known as Old Frontenac, all of which is on the National Register of Historic Places. In between Frontenac and Old Frontenac is **Frontenac State Park.** If you'd like a more in-depth nature experience, plan extended visiting time here. The park is especially valuable for birdwatchers, with over 250 species of birds recorded on-site, and buffalo are occasionally spotted. Camping, hiking, and a winter sliding hill are among the amenities spread across the park's prairie, forest, and river bluff settings.

Not far from Frontenac is **Lake City,** also on the shores of Lake Pepin and home to **Lake City Marina,** the Mississippi's largest recreational marina. A notable piece of Lake City history: waterskiing was invented here by Ralph Samuelson in 1922. The city's main park, **Hok-Si-La Park,** is a 250-

*Old Frontenac.*

acre lakeside park run by the city, offering impressive views across the lake as well as sandy beaches, a mile-long trail along the Mississippi, and tent camping. Nearby is Nosh, an upscale, trendy Mediterranean-based restaurant. Whenever possible, the chefs source locally for their foods, bringing a Midwest theme in as well. The main courses are spectacular, but an excellent meal can be had off the eatery's small plates menu. Save room for dessert.

## IN THE AREA

### Accommodations

**The Candlelight Inn,** 818 West Third Street, Red Wing. Call 651-388-8034; 800-254-9194. Website: www.candlelightinn-redwing.com.

**Classic Rosewood Inn,** 315 Pine Street, Hastings. Call 651-437-3297. Website: www.thorwoodinn.com.

**The Golden Lantern Inn,** 721 East Avenue, Red Wing. Call 651-388-3315; 888-288-3315. Website: www.goldenlantern.com.

**Guesthouse Next Door,** 1117 West 4th Street, Red Wing. Call 651-388-8145; 866-388-8145. Website: www.moondanceinn.com/guesthouse.

**Moondance Inn,** 1105 West 4th Street, Red Wing. Call 651-388-8145; 866-388-8145. Website: www.moondanceinn.com/index.html.

**Round Barn Farm,** 28650 Wild-wood Lane, Red Wing. Call 651-385-9250; 866-763-2276. Website: www.roundbarnfarm.com.

**The St. James Hotel,** 406 Main Street, Red Wing. Call 800-252-1875. Website: www.st-james-hotel.com.

## Attractions and Recreation

**Alexis Bailly Vineyard,** 18200 Kirby Avenue, Hastings. Call 651-437-1413. Website: www.abvwines.com.

**Antiques on Main,** 205 East Second Street, Hastings. Call 651-480-8192.

**The Briar Patch,** 103 East Second Street, Hastings. Call 651-437-4400.

The St. James Hotel, Red Wing.

**Cannon Valley Trail,** Cannon Falls. Call 507-263-0508. Website: www.cannonvalleytrail.com.

**Carpenter St. Croix Valley Nature Center,** 12805 St. Croix Trail South, Hastings. Call 651-437-4359. Website: http://carpenternaturecenter.org/.

**The Emporium,** 213 East Second Street, Hastings. Call 651-438-5444. Website: www.theemporiumofhastings.com.

**Frontenac State Park,** 29223 CR 28 Boulevard, Frontenac. Call 651-345-3401. Website: www.dnr.state.mn.us/state_parks/frontenac/index.html.

**Goodhue County Historical Society,** 1166 Oak Street, Red Wing. Call 651-388-6024. Website: www.goodhuehistory.mus.mn.us.

**Hok-Si-La-Park,** 2500 North MN 61, Lake City. Call 6541-345-3855.

**Lake City Marina,** 201 South Franklin Street, Lake City. Call 651-345-4211.

**The LeDuc House,** 1629 Vermillion Street, Hastings. Call 651-437-7055. Website: www.dakotahistory.org/LeDuc/home.asp.

**Mississippi Clayworks,** 214 East Second Street, Hastings. Call 651-437-5901. Website: www.mississippiclayworks.com.

**Pottery Place Historic Center,** MN 61, Red Wing. Call 612-822-0367. Website: www.rwpotteryplace.com.

**Red Wing Shoe Museum,** 315 Main Street, Red Wing. Call 651-388-6233.

**Scandinavian Marketplace,** 218 East Second Street, Hastings. Call 651-438-9183.

**Sheldon Theatre,** 443 West 3rd Street, Red Wing. Call 651-388-8700; 800-899-5759. Website: www.sheldontheatre.org.

**Treasure Island Resort and Casino,** 5734 Sturgeon Lake Road, Welch. Call 800-222-7077. Website: www.treasureislandcasino.com.

**Vermillion Falls Park,** MN 61 and 21st Street East, Hastings.

**Welch Village,** 26685 CR 7 Boulevard, Welch. Call 651-258-4567. Website: www.welchvillage.com.

## Dining

**Current on the Mississippi,** 101 East 2nd Street, Hastings. 651-437-4814. Website: www.mississippibelle.net.

**Levee Café,** 100 Sibley Street, Hastings. Call 651-437-7577.

**Liberty's,** 303 West 3rd Street, Red Wing. Call 651-388-8877. Website: www.libertysonline.com.

**Lily's Coffee House & Flowers,** 419 West 3rd Street, Red Wing. Call 651-388-8797.

**Nosh,** 310 South Washington Street, Lake City. Call 651-345-2425. Website: www.noshrestaurant.com.

**Oar d'oeuvre,** 433 Main Street, Red Wing. Call 651-388-2155.

**The Port Restaurant** and the **Veranda,** both in the St. James Hotel, 406 Main Street, Red Wing. Call 800-252-1875. Website: www.st-james-hotel.com.

## Other Contacts

**Hastings Area Chamber of Commerce,** 111 East 3rd Street, Hastings. Call 651-437-6775; 888-612-6122. Website: www.hastingsmn.org.

**Lake City Chamber of Commerce,** 101 West Center Street, Lake City. Call 651-345-4123. Website: www.lakecity.org.

**Red Wing Convention and Visitors Bureau,** 420 Levee Street, Red Wing. Call 651-385-5934; 800-498-3444. Website: www.redwing.org.

*Trailhead at John A. Latsch State Park.*

CHAPTER

11

# La Crescent to Wabasha: Apple Blossoms and River Towns

**Estimated length:** 70 miles
**Estimated time:** 2 hours

**Getting there:** From the Twin Cities, take I-494 to MN 55, then take MN 56 to MN 61. Follow MN 61 to La Crescent.

**Highlights:** The short but lovely Apple Blossom Scenic Drive; the views from Great River Bluff State Park; the Museum of Marine Art in Winona; the National Eagle Center in Wabasha; and the steep (but worthwhile) bluff climb at John A. Latsch State Park. Note: this could be combined with the Northern Mississippi Bluff Country route (Chapter 10) for a longer trip.

The southeastern corner of the state, bordered by the mighty Mississippi to the east, has some of the loveliest terrain in Minnesota: river valleys, rolling hills, woods and wildflowers in-season, and one charming small town after the other, including some of the oldest towns in the state, most with many intact historic buildings and landmarks. Unlike more northern reaches, which were leveled and redesigned during the last ice age, the bluff country mostly escaped the glacial ravages and kept instead a variable terrain that includes 500-foot limestone bluffs and deep valleys. The climate here is slightly different too, warmer and with more rainfall, leading to vegetation not seen elsewhere in the state, including black walnut trees. The region is also home to Minnesota's only poisonous snakes, the timber rattlesnake and the massasauga, which reside mostly in the bluffs themselves or in the swampy areas close to the river. But these snakes are as timid of humans as we are of them, and are slow to strike.

Bike trails abound, many of which are paved and can be used for cross-country skiing in the winter months. The state parks along the way offer hiking trails that provide expansive views of the Mississippi and neighboring Wisconsin.

The driving route involves the southeastern Minnesota section of the **Great River Road National Scenic Byway,** a nearly 575-mile route that travels with the Mississippi within the state up to its origins in Itasca State Park. South of Minnesota, of course, the Byway extends all the way to Louisiana. If you were to take the time to follow the entire Minnesota route, you would see a wide variety of scenery as the landscape changes from north to south; for this route, you'll see some of the most striking river bluff scenery in the state.

Starting in La Crescent, you can pick up the **Apple Blossom Scenic Drive** by following County Route 29 (CR 29, also known as North Elm Street) just outside the city center. Shortly after starting the Drive, the road crosses county lines and becomes CR 1, eventually turning into CR 12 before you arrive in Nodine. Continue north on CR 12 until you reach CR 3, then follow that back to MN 61 to complete the Drive.

This short (only 17 miles) but lovely drive takes you through rolling hills filled with apple orchards. Spring and early summer are great choices for visiting, when the trees are in full blossom, but don't discount the beauty that fall brings when the leaves change. Fall is also a great time to shop along the Drive, as orchard owners sell not only apples and apple goods like cider and pastries, but pumpkins as well. Even winter is a good time to explore the Drive, with blankets of snow providing a serene backdrop for the arrival of the winter birds.

Toward the end of the Apple Blossom Scenic Drive, you'll reach **Great River Bluffs State Park,** the entrance to which is on CR 3. The park itself is within the **Richard J. Dorer Memorial Hardwood Forest** and contains acres of red and white pine, maple-basswood, old hickory, and ash trees, as well as areas of "goat prairie," or dry prairie, a low-moisture grassland with bedrock beneath that is not hospitable to trees. It has two Scientific Nature Areas, King's and Queen's Bluffs. King's Bluff is a popular hiking trail, especially for birders: the spectacular overlook of the Mississippi is a great spot to see eagles and hawks. Hiking in the warmer months and cross-country skiing, snowshoeing, and skate-skiing in the winter keep this park busy year-round.

Follow CR 3 north to MN 61 and continue driving northwest to CR 7. Turning onto CR 7 will bring you to the little town of Pickwick, home of the **Pickwick Mill.** The mill, which operated as both a gristmill and a sawmill, opened shortly before the Civil War and ran 24 hours a day during the war before settling into life as a flour mill afterward. Its multiple floors are open to the public, with self-guided tours that explain the function of each floor. The location, right on Big Trout Creek, makes a great stop for a picnic.

Returning to MN 61 and resuming the northern track, take another detour just south of Winona when you reach US 14. Just off MN 61 is the **Bunnell House,** a Gothic Revival house built in the 1850s by the Bunnells,

*The Bunnell House, Homer.*

a pioneer and fur-trading family who enjoyed the natural habitat around them, canoeing and building friendly relationships with the local Native Americans. Its white pine siding has never been painted, giving it a starkly weathered look.

Shortly after leaving the Bunnell House, you'll arrive in **Winona**. The city of Winona is defined by water: its northern boundary is dictated by the Mississippi River, and its southern boundary is formed by Lake Winona. The city itself is on a sandbar.

Winona's name came from the Dakota name We-No-Nah, or firstborn daughter. Legend has it that We-No-Nah was a Dakota girl who committed suicide after not being allowed to marry the man of her desire. There is a statue in her honor in the city's center.

Winona's history is rooted in shipping, not a surprise given its location. Founded in 1851, it was already a bustling river town when the railroad

Lake Winona.

arrived in 1862, further enhancing the city's prominence as a center of business and agriculture. By 1900, Winona had more millionaires per capita than any other city in the United States.

Although times have changed and Winona isn't as economically prosperous as it was a century ago, historically it's a treasure trove for visitors. Downtown Winona has more than one hundred buildings listed on the National Register of Historic Places, most built between 1857 and 1916 in Italianate or Queen Anne style. The best way to take in this large collection of Victorian commercial buildings (the largest concentration in Minnesota) is by foot. Free walking tour brochures of the district are available from the visitors center on Huff Street, immediately after you turn right off MN 61 (and which, being right on the shores of Lake Winona, is a good spot for a picnic too).

More history can be found at the **Winona County Historical Museum,** which underwent an expansion in 2010. A large and fascinating collection of local and regional historic exhibits, covering the usual (geologic history, river trade) as well as the less so (Cold War parking plans in the event of nuclear war). The museum is kid-friendly, with lots of hands-on activities, including a climb-through cave and river steamboat, all in an intriguing and architecturally eclectic building reflecting both Winona's past and present.

The **Arches Museum of Pioneer Life** is a tribute to the long-lost days of roadside museums. It contains the collection of Walter Rahn, who apparently was fascinated with pioneer life and either collected or built items himself to illustrate their uses. The grounds also have a log cabin and a one-room schoolhouse.

The **Polish Cultural Institute** pays homage to the point in history when Winona had the largest concentration of Polish immigrants in the United States. The museum reflects that heritage with antiques, folk art, religious items, and displays detailing the immigrants' experience.

One of Winona's prominent employers is J.R. Watkins, the maker of natural home care, remedy, and food products and flavorings. The company has been in Winona since 1868, and its history is on display at the **Watkins Museum and Store,** housed in the company's former print shop in its large manufacturing complex.

A newer gem is the **Minnesota Marine Art Museum.** This attractive museum, opened in 2006, is located along the Mississippi and has an extensive collection of marine art, folk art, photography, maps, and historical

## THE STAINED-GLASS CAPITAL

At the peak of its economic history, Winona was full of millionaires, and those looking to use their discretionary income to build were fond of stained glass. Consequently, Winona has a dozen elaborate buildings, both commercial and religious, that have striking stained-glass collections. Even though most builders no longer use this beautiful (and expensive) architectural adornment, the city also has several stained-glass studios with contemporary craftsmen creating and restoring stained-glass pieces around the United States. To see examples of the historical stained glass, you can visit the **J.R. Watkins Company, Merchants National Bank, Winona National Bank** (which also has the **African Safari Museum,** collected by the bank's original owner, inside), the **Church of St. Stanislaus Kostka,** and **Chapel of St. Mary of the Angels.** Two prominent studios working in stained glass today include the **Hauser Art Glass Co.,** the largest stained-glass company in the United States, and **Cathedral Crafts,** both of which offer group tours with advance arrangements. The Winona Visitor Center has a brochure detailing the stained glass locations.

displays, all highlighting the diversity of marine life. The permanent collection includes pieces by artists like Homer, Renoir, and Monet. Be sure to slow down as you're driving to and from the museum, so you can enjoy the eclectic groups of houseboats clustered along the river.

Winona has several city parks, some of which are of special interest. **Windom Park** is small, only a city block in size, but it's surrounded by several Victorian houses (some of which are listed on the National Register of Historic Places) and has a gazebo and fountain with the sculpture of Princess We-No-Nah. **Lake Park,** on the shores of Lake Winona, is a popular city park with an attractive rose garden (C. A. Rohrer Rose Garden), fishing piers, and a band shell with weekly live concerts during the summer. Just outside downtown Winona is **Garvin Heights City Park,** nearly 600 feet above the city, offering wide-ranging views of Winona and the river.

Like so many of the river towns in the state, Winona has some lovely historic bed & breakfasts. The **Alexander Mansion Bed and Breakfast** has four elaborately detailed Victorian rooms, all with private bath, and including five-course breakfast and evening hors d'oeuvres. The 1886 mansion also has an extensive screened porch for guests to enjoy. The **Carriage House Bed and Breakfast** was built by lumber baron Conrad Bohn, and the Carriage House was literally that—it originally housed six carriages and several horses. Today the renovated house has four bedrooms, all with private baths, decorated in a cozy Victorian style. Breakfast is included daily, as is the use of single and tandem bicycles and, by prearrangement, a Model A Ford for local touring. The **Windom Park Bed and Breakfast,** located near Windom Park, is a Colonial Revival house built in 1900 and has four beautiful rooms in the main house, all with private bath, and two lofts in the nearby carriage house. The lofts have fireplaces and two-person Jacuzzis. Breakfast is included each day, and guests are encouraged to use the other public rooms, which are also impeccably appointed.

There are plenty of places to get a good meal too. **Signatures** is one of the more upscale restaurants in the area, while **Betty Jo Byoloski's** is a more casual alternative, serving burgers, soups, and chili. **Green Mill** may be a chain, but the deep-dish pizza is worth a visit. **Jefferson Pub & Grill** offers a solid pub menu.

Just outside downtown Winona is **Garvin Heights Vineyards,** which you can reach by following Huff Street back to and across MN 61, where Huff Street turns into CR 44, or Garvin Heights Road. Garvin Heights makes wine from locally grown grapes, including some grown at the vineyard. Besides grapes, they use raspberries and cranberries. The vineyard's tasting room is open seasonally.

Shortly after departing Winona on MN 61, another side trip is possible at MN 248. Turn left onto the state highway and travel about 3 miles, to CR 25, or State Street. You've arrived in the little town of Rollingstone, and turning onto Main Street will bring you to the **Rollingstone Luxembourg Heritage Museum.** The town of Rollingstone was founded by members of Luxembourg's Grand Duchy in the mid-1800s, and at one point was the largest settlement of Luxembourg emigrants in the country. The Rollingstone Luxembourg Heritage Museum pays tribute to that history in the former city hall and fire station, built in 1900.

A few miles north of the Rollingstone exit on MN 61 is **John A. Latsch State Park.** One of the lesser-visited state parks, this is worth a trip if you're ready for some exercise; there's .5-mile stairway hike up to the top of bluffs that leads to outstanding views of the Mississippi and surrounding bluffs.

The final leg of this journey brings you through **Kellogg** and **Wabasha,** two of the oldest towns on the upper Mississippi, with the latter having been founded in 1826 and Kellogg shortly after that. One of Wabasha's claims to fame is as the setting for the movies *Grumpy Old Men* and

## THE NATIONAL EAGLE CENTER

*National Eagle Center, Wabasha.*

The **National Eagle Center,** located on the Mississippi River banks, is a 14,000-square-foot interpretive center with resident eagles, a viewing deck, housing for injured or sick eagles, exhibits with preserved animals and other artifacts, and demonstration and classroom areas. Five "superstars," or rescued eagles from around the country, are cared for in a sanctuary environment and give visitors a close-up view of these majestic creatures. The Wabasha area counts more than one hundred bald eagles as year-round residents, and thousands more migrate through the region between October and April. Every autumn the NEC holds a special "deck opening" event to mark the arrival of bald eagles for the winter; this area of the Mississippi has one of the largest concentrations of bald eagles in the contiguous United States.

*Grumpier Old Men.* But it has several other amenities that are equally valuable and entertaining (if not more so), one of which is the population of eagles that can be found year-round, but particularly in the winter.

River activities are popular in Wabasha. Houseboat and pontoon rentals can be arranged through **Great River Houseboats,** or you can enjoy a sunset or moonlight sail aboard the 31-foot sailboat *The Messenger.*

Fun of a different kind can be found in Kellogg's **Lark Toys.** This massive toy complex (more than 30,000 square feet) is more than just a store, it's a playground. A working carousel offers rides, and a mini-golf course is available during the warmer months. LARK stands for "Lost Art Revival by Kreofsky," and vintage toys, many made out of wood, are produced and sold here, along with children's books. A café is on-site.

A visit to the **Arrowhead Bluffs Museum** is a must for hunting enthusiasts. The museum has a large collection of mounted wildlife specimens as well as pioneer and Native American artifacts, and it also has a complete collection of Winchester guns manufactured from 1866 to 1982.

Just north of Wabasha on MN 61 is the **Wabasha County Historical Museum.** This small museum on the second floor of a former schoolhouse is not necessarily the most comprehensive historical museum in the state, but it does have some items of interest to fans of Laura Ingalls Wilder.

Lodging options abound. **America's Lofts of Wabasha** offers full condos with fireplaces, kitchens, and Jacuzzis. For bed & breakfast enthusiasts, the **River Nest Bed & Breakfast** is a newer construction offering two private suites, both overlooking the river, while **American Eagle Bluff Bed and Breakfast** is in a secluded forest overlooking the Mississippi and Chippewa Rivers, with just two guest suites with private baths.

Dining presents a number of good options as well. **Vinifera** doesn't just have fine dining and a wine bar, it has a patio overlooking the river. Also offering river views and boat-in dining is **Slippery's**, which was mentioned in the *Grumpy Old Men* movies. Burgers, steaks, and Mexican items are served in hearty portions. The **Olde Triangle Pub** is a casual, friendly neighborhood spot with good pub grub, including bangers and mash and Irish stew.

## IN THE AREA

### Accommodations

**Alexander Mansion Bed and Breakfast,** 274 East Broadway, Winona. Call: 507-474-4224. Website: www.alexandermansionbb.com.

**America's Lofts of Wabasha,** 152 West Main Street, Wabasha. Full condos with fireplaces, kitchens, and Jacuzzis. Call: 651-565-3509. Website: www.eaglesontheriver.com.

**American Eagle Bluff Bed and Breakfast,** Read's Landing. Call 651-564-0372. Website: www.americaneaglebluffbedandbreakfast.com.

**Carriage House Bed and Breakfast,** 420 Main Street, Winona. Call 507-452-8256. Website: www.chbb.com.

**The River Nest Bed & Breakfast,** 20073 CR 77, Reads Landing. Call 651-560-4077. Website: www.therivernest.com.

**Windom Park Bed and Breakfast,** 3369 West Broadway, Winona. Call 507-457-9515; 866-737-1719. Website: www.windompark.com.

## Attractions and Recreation

**Arches Museum of Pioneer Life,** US 14. Call 507-523-2111. Website: www.winonahistory.org.

**Arrowhead Bluffs Museum,** 17505 667th Street, Wabasha. Call 651-565-3829.

**Bunnell House,** MN 61 and US 14, Homer. Call 507-452-7575. Website: www.winonahistory.org.

**Chapel of St. Mary of the Angels,** 1155 West Wabasha, Winona. Call 507-453-5550. Website: www.smumn.edu/chapel.aspx.

**Church of St. Stanislaus Kostka,** 625 East 4th Street, Winona. Call 507-452-5430.

**Downtown National Register of Historic Places District.** Free walking tour brochures available from the Convention and Visitors Bureau, the visitors center at 924 Huff Street, or the Winona County Historical Society.

**Garvin Heights City Park,** Garvin Heights Rd, Winona.

**Garvin Heights Vineyards,** 2255 Garvin Heights Road, Winona. Call 507-313-1917. Website: www.ghvwine.com.

**Great River Bluffs State Park,** 43605 Kipp Drive, Winona. Call 507-643-6859. Website: www.dnr.state.mn.us/state_parks/great_river_bluffs/index.html.

*Great River Bluffs State Park.*

**Great River Houseboats,** 125 Beach Harbor Road, Alma, Wisconsin. Call 651-798-4411. Website: www.greatriverhouseboats.moonfruit.com.

**John A. Latsch State Park,** 43605 Kipp Drive, Winona. Call 507-643-6849. Website: www.dnr.state.mn.us/state_parks/john_latsch/index.html.

**Lake Park,** 900 Huff Street, Winona.

**LARK Toys,** MN 61, Kellogg. Call 507-767-3387. Website: www.larktoys.com.

**Merchants National Bank,** 102 East Third Street, Winona. Call 507-457-1100. Website: www.merchantsbank.com.

**The Messenger,** 137 West Main Street, Wabasha. Call 651-565-4158. Website: www.wabashamn.org.

**Minnesota Marine Art Museum,** 800 Riverview Drive, Winona. Call 507-474-6626; 866-940-6626. Website: www.minnesotamarineart.org.

**National Eagle Center,** 50 Pembroke Avenue, Wabasha. Call 651-565-4989; 877-332-4537. Website: www.nationaleaglecenter.org.

**Pickwick Mill,** 26421 CR 7, Pickwick. Call 507-457-0499. Website: www.pickwickmill.org.

**Polish Museum of Minnesota,** 102 Liberty Street, Winona. Call 507-454-3431. Website: www.polishmuseumwinona.org.

**Rollingstone Luxembourg Heritage Museum,** 98 Main Street, Rollingstone. Call 507-689-2307. Website: www.luxamculturalsociety.org/RollingstoneLuxHeritageMuseum.htm.

**Wabasha County Historical Society Museum,** US 61, Reads Landing. Call 651-345-3987.

**Watkins Museum and Store,** 150 Liberty Street, Winona. Call 507-457-6095.

**Windom Park,** Huff and West Broadway Street, Winona.

**Winona County History Center,** 160 Johnson Street, Winona. Call 507-454-2723. Website: www.winonahistory.org.

**Winona National Bank,** 204 Main Street, Winona. Call 507-454-4320. Website: www.winonanationalbank.com.

## Dining

**Betty Jo Byoloski's,** 66 Center Street, Winona. Call 507-454-2687. This casual neighborhood institution, packed full of historical artifacts, serves up burgers and pasta in hearty portions at reasonable prices. Website: www.bettyjos.com.

**Green Mill,** 1025 US 61, Winona. The deep-dish pizza is the chain's specialty. Call 507-452-5400. Website: www.greenmill.com.

**Jefferson Pub & Grill,** 58 Center Street, Winona. Hearty pub sandwiches and soups. Call 507-452-2718. Website: www.jeffersonpub.com.

**Signatures,** 22852 CR 17, Winona. The food here is excellent, and you can feast on the outdoor views out of the generous windows. Call 507-454-3767. Website: www.signatureswinona.com.

**Slippery's,** 10 Church Avenue, Wabasha. Call 866-504-4036. Seafood and steaks served in hearty portions in a restaurant with great views of the river. Website: www.slipperysumr.com.

**The Olde Triangle Pub,** 219 Main Street, Wabasha. Call 651-565-0256. A casual, friendly neighborhood spot with good pub grub, including bangers and mash and Irish stew. Website: www.oldetrianglepub.com.

**Vinifera,** 260 Main Street West, Wabasha. A seasonally changing fine-dining menu accompanied by an outstanding international wine list. Call 651-565-4171. Website: viniferarestaurant.com.

## Other Contacts

**Apple Blossom Scenic Drive,** La Crescent. Website: www.byways.org/explore/byways/2238/.

**Convention and Visitors Bureau,** 160 Johnson Street. Call 507-452-0735; 800-657-4972. This is a duplicate of what I already put in below. They're branding as Visit Winona.

**Visit Winona,** 160 Johnson Street, Winona. Call 800-657-4972. Website: www.visitwinona.com.

**Wabasha Kellogg Chamber of Commerce,** 137 West Main Street, Wabasha. Call 800-565-4158. Website: www.wabashamn.org.

**Winona County Historical Society,** 160 Johnson Street, Wabasha. Call 507-454-2723.

*The Falls in Minneopa State Park.*

CHAPTER

12

# Minnesota River Valley, Part 1: Carver to Mankato

**Estimated length:** 55 miles
**Estimated time:** 2 hours

**Getting there:** From Carver, take County Route 40 (CR 40) to just north of Belle Plaine, then continue on CR 6 to Henderson. CR 6 then becomes MN 93, traveling to Le Sueur, where you can pick up US 169 south to Mankato.

**Highlights:** The Hooper-Bowler Hillstrom House with its "unique" architectural features; the charming small river town of Henderson; the birthplace of both the founder of the Mayo Clinic and the Jolly Green Giant; Minneopa State Park, with its gorgeous trails and waterfall; and Mankato, home to both literary and sports icons.

Leaving the Twin Cities to explore the Minnesota River Valley is a lovely way to spend an afternoon. The Minnesota River was formed by glaciers during the last North American ice age, roughly ten thousand years ago. Today it flows southeast from Big Stone Lake in the western edge of the state, near the North and South Dakota borders, until it reaches Mankato, when it redirects northeast until it meets the Mississippi near the Twin Cities. It's an area full of changes, from closely wooded stretches along rolling riverbanks to wide-open prairie spaces. It's also full of history, perhaps most notably the Dakota Conflict of 1862, numerous Native American sites, and the homes of some iconic Minnesota people and companies, including the founder of the Mayo Clinic and the hometown of the Jolly Green Giant.

The part of the river covered in this trip starts just southwest of the Twin Cities and ends in Mankato, although it could be combined with the New Ulm to Fort Ridgely leg to make a longer trip. When you look at a map, it appears that taking US 169 from the Twin Cities is the logical road choice, as it's the major road heading in that direction. It's faster, that's true, but although scenic in its own way, the parallel county routes recommended here are more rewarding, even if they do force you to slow down. Although that may be the point!

From Carver, take CR 40 south heading to Belle Plaine. Just before you reach Belle Plaine, the road will change to CR 6 as you cross a county line. This short stretch of road winds through woods and gently rolling landscape before arriving in **Belle Plaine,** where you'll turn left onto North Walnut Street. A right turn onto West State Street will bring you to the **Hooper-Bowler-Hillstrom House.** The former home of State Bank founder Samuel Bowler, this house was built in 1871, but its primary claim to fame, besides being an attractive version of a 19th-century house, is the addition Mr. Bowler added to accommodate his rather large family: a two-story outhouse. A skyway connects the second floor of the "five-holer" to the house; the upstairs facilities are situated farther back, so the waste landed behind the wall of the first floor. Although the home has limited visiting hours, it's worth a stop if it works on your schedule, as the house is packed full of antiques and oddities.

Continue on West State Street, which will merge back onto CR 6. At this point, the road is the journey itself, slow and winding as it follows the curves of the Minnesota River. As you approach CR 5, look for its telltale rows of cottonwood trees, known as the Avenue of Trees, that leads east on CR 5 to the Blakely Bridge. The bridge is often the victim of spring floods from the Minnesota River.

Continuing south on CR 6, you'll soon see **St. Thomas Church** on the right. The small, pristine white church was built in 1870 and is now on the National Register of Historic Places, and thought to be a marker of the first Irish agrarian settlement in the state.

The road winds into **Henderson,** a small, New England-y Minnesota River town. At one time, Henderson served as a stopping point for stagecoaches and steamboats; today, shoppers browse for antiques and stop for lunch at the **BitterSweet Café.** There is plenty of history to explore, too; the **Sibley County Historical Museum** displays items immigrants brought with them from Europe, while the **Joseph R. Brown Minnesota River Center** showcases Minnesota River Valley history. A new addition to Main Street is the **Minnesota Valley Mini-Birding Museum,** which educates visitors about the vast number of birds to be seen in the area. A hearty dinner can be had at the **Hog Wild,** especially for those who like ribs, and a complete getaway can be accomplished by booking a stay at the **Henderson House Bed & Breakfast,** on a hill overlooking Main Street.

From Henderson, travel on MN 93 south to **Le Sueur.** Le Sueur is the original home of the Minnesota Canning Company—better known today as Green Giant. The iconic Jolly Green Giant is memorialized on a historic marker at Commerce and Dakota Streets. But the tall green fellow is not the only person of historical interest in town. The founder of the internationally renowned Mayo Clinic also got his start here. The **W.W. Mayo House,** a little gothic-style house hand built in 1859 by Dr. Mayo himself is now open as a museum. Mayo initially set up shop on the second floor. The Civil War interrupted his practice; he traveled to New Ulm to help with wounded veterans while his wife, Louise, remained in the house to shelter 11

*The Minnesota River, outside of Henderson.*

refugee families. By 1864, the Mayo family reunited and moved to Rochester, where they founded the Mayo Clinic. The home's story doesn't end there; in the 1870s, the Carson Nesbit Cosgrove family moved into the home. Cosgrove founded the Minnesota Valley Canning Company, which later became Green Giant.

Additional community history can be explored at the **Le Sueur City Museum.** A small museum in a former schoolhouse, the City Museum has most of what remains of the Green Giant legacy, after Pillsbury bought Green Giant and moved its headquarters out of town. The Green Giant history room has a wide variety of memorabilia and antiques. Other displays include an old-time drugstore and an antique doll collection. If you're in the mood for a longer visit, the **Cosgrove House** is a beautiful, century-old Victorian home with four rooms, all with private bath, and a full breakfast daily.

The next stop is via US 169 south to **Traverse des Sioux,** just a mile north of St. Peter. This shallow river crossing spot served as a gathering point for Native Americans for decades, followed by European traders. A treaty signed in 1851 led to a torrent of white settlers, and a town with the Traverse name soon came into being, but when neighboring St. Peter was named county seat, Traverse des Sioux was all but deserted. A self-guided trail guides visitors through the area and explains the culture and history of its past.

Continue south on US 169 to **St. Peter.** The little town on the river was the center of some extreme political maneuvering in 1857, when a bill was introduced to move the state's capitol from St. Paul to St. Peter, which at the time was a more convenient location for remote legislators. However, not all legislators approved of the idea, and money and real estate no doubt played a part. Finally, a rogue senator physically took the bill and hid out in a local hotel, drinking and gambling, until the deadline for signing it into law had passed.

St. Peter has other facets of historical significance too. E. St. Julien Cox was a Civil War officer, attorney, and eventually state senator, and he built a flamboyant Gothic/Italianate home in 1871. Filled with 1880s furnishings, the **E. St. Julien Cox House** is open to the public today during the summer, when costumed guides explain the significance of both the home and the family.

Another point of history worth revisiting is on display at the **Treaty Site History Center.** The center has permanent and seasonal exhibitions detailing the creation of what is now southern Minnesota, along with Iowa and South Dakota, in the signing of the Traverse des Sioux Treaty in 1851. History aficionados will note that the terms of the treaty were not upheld, leading to the Dakota Conflict several years later. The center doesn't shy away from the uglier side of the history, but if you need something more peaceful and soothing, take some time to explore the restored prairie that surrounds the center.

A final piece of history worth visiting (and planning ahead for, as it's only open to visitors by appointment) is the **St. Peter Regional Treatment Center.** Built in 1866 to serve as a psychiatric facility, the center has since expanded and is still in operation, but the "old" center is a museum that explores how the mentally ill were diagnosed and treated more than a century ago.

**Mankato** is the next stop continuing south on US 169. Mankato is the fourth-largest city in the state and is the county seat. Named as a rough translation of the Dakota's *Makato Osa Watapa,* or "river where blue earth is gathered." The Blue Earth River runs through the city, which is where it joins the Minnesota River.

The city's history is open for exploration at the **Blue Earth Heritage Center.** The museum of the Blue Earth County Historical Society has wide-ranging exhibits covering local historic events, including a Maud Hart Lovelace exhibit, displays featuring Native American artifacts, remnants from the region's early days of farming and milling, and a diorama of old Mankato.

The community, like many others in the region, had rocky relationships with its Native American inhabitants. In 1862, 38 Dakota Indians were hanged in Mankato. Near that site is now a 6-foot, 2-ton statue of a **Dakota Warrior,** part of 1987's "Year of Reconciliation" as mandated by then governor Rudy Perpich.

## ANTIQUING IN MANKATO

As befits a historic region, Mankato has a thriving antique community. If searching out special items with historic interest suits you, be sure to spend some time at the **Historic Old Town District** along North Riverfront Drive. There are several great antiques shops in the district, many housed in historic buildings, including **Old Town Antiques & Mercantile, Little Red Shed, Antiques Etc.,** and **Riverfront Antiques**. Other options for antiquing are **Earthly Remains, Generations Antiques,** and **Willard's Colonial House Antiques.**

Some famous Minnesota authors had homes here as well. Well-loved Maud Hart Lovelace, author of the popular Betsy-Tacy-Tib books, grew up in Mankato and based the books on her childhood. The **Betsy-Tacy Society** gives fans of the book the opportunity to visit the sites of the fictional Deep Valley. Tacy's home is open for tours; Betsy's house is around the corner. The society also has a brochure detailing 55 important stops in Mankato for Betsy-Tacy fans; the map was created in part by Lovelace herself. Check the society's website for the detailed walking map, and call ahead for driving directions. Another notable author, Nobel Prize–winning **Sinclair Lewis,** had a summer home in town. While it is not open to the public, fans can view the exterior at 315 South Broad Street.

Sports fans converge on Mankato each summer, just in time for the **Minnesota Vikings Training Camp.** When the Vikings begin to gear up for the season in July, they start out in Mankato. Practices are free, while admission is charged for scrimmages and games. Get tickets in advance from the Vikings ticket office or from the Mankato Chamber of Commerce (listed at the end of this chapter).

For anyone wanting to spend time outdoors, Mankato has some wonderful options. The **Sakatah Singing Hills State Trail** is a 39-mile paved trail utilizing a former railroad bed that winds from Mankato to Faribault through farmland and woods. From Mankato, take MN 22 north to access public parking. The trail is multiuse, open to all forms of recreation (with the exception of snowmobiles with studded tracks—regular snowmobiles are welcome). A secondary trail is available for horseback riders only.

Just west of Mankato on MN 68 is **Minneopa State Park.** In the Dakota language, *Minneopa* means "water falling twice," a perfect name for this park, home to Minnesota's largest waterfall. A winding trail leads to and around the falls, with a limestone stairway descending into the valley, and out into native prairie grasses. Seppmann Mill, a wind-driven gristmill made of stone and wood, is no longer functional but continues to draw admir-

*Minneopa State Park.*

ers. At one time there was a town here as well, but three consecutive years of grasshopper plagues in the 1870s drove the residents away. Tourists, however, continue to flock to this popular park, for the waterfalls and for the hiking/cross-country skiing trails and bird-watching. Campsites and one cabin are available for rental.

Mankato also has opportunities for some fine dining. The **Wine Café** offers tasty food, but it also has a full bar, including 70 wines by the glass and a comparable number of beers. **Whiskey River** is a congenial supper club with traditional supper club foods, including ribs, steak, and walleye. Perhaps one of the most charming bistros in town is the **Neighbor's Italian Bistro,** which has excellent Italian dishes. When available, try the butternut squash ravioli with maple sage butter and bacon.

If staying in Mankato is an option, good choices include the **Butler House Bed & Breakfast,** a grander-than-average historic mansion that offers five rooms, all with private bath and full breakfast. A more traditional hotel experience can be found at the **Hilton Garden Inn,** near the Minnesota River downtown.

## IN THE AREA

### Accommodations

**Butler House Bed & Breakfast,** 704 South Broad Street, Mankato. Call 507-387-5055. Website: www.butlerhouse.com.

**Cosgrove House,** 228 South 2nd Street, Le Sueur. Call 507-665-2500.

**Henderson House Bed & Breakfast,** 104 North Eighth Street, Henderson. Call 507-248-3356. Website: www.hendersonhouseinnbb.com.

**Hilton Garden Inn,** 20 Civic Center Plaza, Mankato. Call 507-344-1111. Website: www.hiltongardeninn.hilton.com.

### Attractions and Recreation

**Betsy-Tacy Houses,** 332-333 Center Street, Mankato. Call 507-345-9777. Website: www.betsy-tacysociety.org/.

**Blue Earth Heritage Center,** 415 Cherry Street, Mankato. Call 507-345-5566. Website: www.bechshistory.com.

**Dakota Warrior,** 100 East Main Street, Mankato.

**Earthly Remains,** 731 South Front Street, Mankato. Call 507-388-5063. One of the largest antique dealers in the city.

**E. St. Julien Cox Home,** 500 North Washington Avenue, St. Peter. Call 507-934-4309. Website: www.nchsmn.org/sites.html.

**Generations Antiques,** 615 South Front Street, Mankato. Call 507-345-7551.

*Hooper Bowler Hillstrom House, Belle Plaine.*

**Hooper-Bowler-Hillstrom House,** 410 North Cedar Street, Belle Plaine. Call 952-873-6109. Website: www .belleplainemn.com/about/Hooper House.php.

**Le Sueur City Museum,** 709 North Second Street, Le Sueur. Call 507-655-2050.

**Minneopa State Park,** 54497 Gadwall Road, Mankato. Call 507-389-5464. Website: www.dnr.state.mn.us/state_parks/minneopa/index.html.

**Minnesota Valley Mini-Birding Museum,** 526 Main Street, Henderson.

**Minnesota Vikings Training Camp,** Blakeslee Field, Minnesota State University. Call 507-389-3000. Website: www.vikings.com.

**St. Peter Regional Treatment Center,** 100 Freeman Drive, St. Peter. Call 507-931-7270.

**Traverse des Sioux,** US 169, 1 mile north of St. Peter. Call 507-934-2160. Website: www.mnhs.org/places/sites/tds/index.html.

**Treaty Site History Center,** 1851 North Minnesota Avenue, St. Peter. Call 507-934-2160. Website: www.nchsmn.org/sites.html.

**Willard's Colonial House Antiques,** 20 Skyline Drive, Mankato. Call 507-387-2400.

**W.W. Mayo House,** 118 North Main Street, Le Sueur. Call 507-665-3250. Website: www.mnhs.org/places/sites/wwmh.

## Dining

**BitterSweet Coffee,** 522 Main Street, Henderson. Call 507-248-3850. Coffee shop with breakfast/lunch menu items.

**Hog Wild Saloon,** 514 Main Street, Henderson. Call 507-248-3173. Prime rib, ribs, burgers, and sandwiches.

**The Neighbor's Italian Bistro,** 1812 South Riverfront Drive, Mankato. Call 507-625-6776. Open daily for lunch and dinner. Excellent Italian bistro with homemade pastas and a thoughtful menu. Website: www .neighborsitalianbistro.com.

**Whiskey River,** 34166 MN 99, Mankato. Call 507-934-5600. Open daily for lunch and dinner, Sat. through Sun. for breakfast. Congenial supper club with traditional supper club foods, including ribs, steak, and walleye. Website: www.riversp.com.

**Wine Café,** 301 North Riverfront, Mankato. Call 507-345-1516. Open Mon. through Sat. for lunch and dinner. A charming bistro with a limited bar menu and wine shop with more than just wine. Website: www.wine cafebar.com.

## Other Contacts

**Belle Plaine Chamber of Commerce.** Call 952-873-4295. Website: www .belleplainemn.com.

**Greater Mankato Convention & Visitors Bureau.** Call 507-385-6660. Website: www.visitgreatermankato.com.

**Henderson, MN.** Website: www.hendersonmn.com.

**Le Sueur Chamber of Commerce,** 500 North Main Street, Le Sueur. Call 507-665-2501. Website: www.lesueurchamber.org.

**St. Peter Area Chamber of Commerce,** 101 South Front Street, St. Peter. Call 507-934-3400.

*New Ulm's Glockenspiel.*

CHAPTER 13

# Minnesota River Valley, Part 2:
## Mankato to Fairfax

**Estimated length:** 55 miles
**Estimated time:** 1.5 hours

**Getting there:** From the Twin Cities, take MN 5 west to Gaylord, when the highway number changes to MN 19. Follow MN 19 to Fairfax, then travel south on County Route 74 (CR 74) to the Fairfax Historical Depot Museum.

**Highlights:** Historical highlights: Fort Ridgely State Park, the Brown County Historical Museum, the Harkin Store, and the John Lind House. Scenic highlights: the lovely drive along the Minnesota River and the beautiful historic town of New Ulm, which includes the gardens at Schell's Brewery and Flandrau State Park.

This is a short but both scenically and historically rich route, and it ends in a river town well worth spending some extra time exploring. You could lengthen it by attaching it to the Pioneer Trails (Chapter 15) and/or the Carver to Mankato route (Chapter 12).

The scenery in this area benefits from having been formed during the last ice age, which left the area full of lakes and wetlands, not to mention the winding, hilly roads around the Minnesota River. It's also rich in Native American and pioneer history, but not all of it is joyful—various points

## FORT RIDGELY STATE PARK

At a little over 1,000 acres, Fort Ridgely State Park isn't one of the state's largest parks, but it's packed with things to do. In its small space are hiking and horse-back riding trails, campsites, fishable waters, a hill appropriately sized for some excellent winter sledding, and a nine-hole golf course. History buffs will want to wander around the remains of Fort Ridgely, which was completed in 1855 and housed three hundred people during its life span (the fort closed in 1872). Its primary purpose was to be not so much a military outpost as a police station, keeping order and protecting the newly arrived white settlers. It was attacked twice during the Dakota Conflict. Today, one of the fort's buildings has been restored and is available for tours, or visitors can wander on their own through the remnants of the other fort buildings. Comprehensive interpretive signs explain what each building was and its significance to the fort. Nearby is a his-toric cemetery, with gravestones and monuments revealing additional informa-tion about the people who lived, fought, and died in the fort. Recent excavations have also uncovered Indian burial mounds and signs of settlements that may date back centuries.

throughout this region witnessed the Dakota Conflict of 1862, when the Dakota people struck out against white settlers in protest of treaty viola-tions and the hunger and deprivation resulting from misdirected or stolen annuities by Indian agents. In the end, innocent people on both sides were killed, and the aftermath of the conflict reverberated through the area for decades. This route visits another important historical site in that war.

The journey begins with a historic site in the small town of Fairfax. The **Fairfax Historical Depot Museum** is a restored railroad depot in Depot Park, full of remnants of Fairfax's rail past as well as pieces of the town's history. Depot Park serves as the beginning of the **FairRidge Trail,** a paved hiking and biking trail that meanders through woodlands and hills before ending at **Fort Ridgely State Park.** Part of the trail has a horseback riding trail running adjacent to it.

From Fort Ridgely, travel southeast on CR 21. This is a winding, hilly stretch of road that at points hugs the Minnesota River and other times twists and turns throughout narrow, tree-lined stretches. Through the trees you might see the twisting river, or more forests, or glimpses of farmland tucked into the valleys, or wetlands. Take your time—around every corner is another beautiful view. If you want to pull over for a closer look or a photo opportunity, park carefully—there are many blind curves. It's beautiful any time of year, but it especially shines in the fall, when the colors change.

Continuing on CR 21, you'll find the **Harkin Store,** a piece of history still vibrant today. The Harkin Store was a community general store until the day the railroad decided to bypass it. The store was forced to close, and today much of the merchandise on display is exactly where it was left the day the store closed. Costumed guides provide historical background and explain what some of the products, common in their day but unknown today, were for. The Harkin Store provides a rare opportunity to see what a general store was really like more than one hundred years ago.

At the intersection of CR 21, CR 15, and US 14, follow US 14 west to **New Ulm.** This charming river city was conceived by German settlers who initially arrived in Chicago in 1853, then planned in advance to build their own community in Minnesota. Besides its location on the river, which

*Harkin General Store, New Ulm.*

made it valuable in the early days of commerce and trading, New Ulm went on to serve another valuable role, as a refuge for people trying to escape the Dakota Conflict. In the 1920s, the town developed another type of infamy, as resident Whoopee John Wilfahrt and his musical magic gave New Ulm the reputation of "polka capital of the nation."

But its German heritage is what is still apparent today, in the architecture, landmarks, and festivals and celebrations that take place each year. One example is the **Glockenspiel.** New Ulm is home to one of the world's few freestanding carillons. The 45-foot glockenspiel puts on its show three times a day, more often during festivals; when the bells chime, 3-foot-tall polka figures dance out, except at Christmas, when a nativity scene appears instead.

In the town itself is the **Hermann Monument.** This towering monument was built in 1897 in honor of Hermann of Cherusci, who is recognized for liberating Germany from Rome in A.D. 9 and is considered the liberator of the German people. The monument was built through the efforts of several chapters of the Sons of Hermann, a fraternal order of German Americans. The memorial stands 102 feet tall and, for those willing to climb the stairs, provides an excellent view of greater New Ulm. Bring a picnic lunch to enjoy in the park grounds.

New Ulm's history is on full display at the **Brown County Historical Museum.** Housed in a 1910 post office, the museum is a surprisingly

---

## AUGUST SCHELL BREWING COMPANY

**Oktoberfest** comes to town every year, due in no small part to the August Schell Brewing Company. Schell's is the second-oldest family brewing company in the United States, having opened in 1860. Having offered hospitality to visiting Dakota, the brewery was largely left alone during the Dakota Conflict. It also remained operational by producing "near beer" and root beer during Prohibition (it still produces root beer, called 1919 after the year the 18th Amendment was passed). Today the brewery is open for tours seasonally (kids welcome—while the adults enjoy a beer tasting at the end, minors and nondrinkers can sample the 1919 root beer), and there's a small museum and gift shop. What's also very much worth a visit is the brewery grounds and gardens. Stop in the spring for the arrival of the bulbs, or midsummer to see the rest of the garden in full bloom. You might even see some wildlife in the adjacent deer park.

*Brown County Museum, New Ulm.*

diverse and comprehensive collection of historic and cultural artifacts and displays. German heritage (including items donated by the German city of Ulm), Native American presence, and the economic mainstays of the area (known as "beer, brats, and bricks") are all detailed in various exhibits. The Dakota Conflict is especially well covered. The building itself is beautiful and worth a visit.

Nearby is the **John Lind House.** Built in 1887, this Victorian beauty served as both home and venue for state functions for Governor John Lind. The house had fallen into serious disrepair before being listed on the National Register and being purchased by the newly formed Lind House Association, which restored it and operates it today. While tours are available, this is still a working building, home to the local United Way.

A more whimsical display about New Ulm's history is on the **Heritage Tree,** a fanciful tree decorated with historic figures from new Ulm's past.

A serene piece of religious history is just outside the historic city center. The **Way of the Cross** was built in 1904 and has 14 stations along a path climbing a hill (of moderate height) depicting the trial and crucifixion of Christ, cresting in the chapel at the top, dedicated to the Mother of Sorrows. The Way of the Cross was renovated in 2004 and is a lovely bit of nature and history tucked into more mundane urban surroundings.

Literary history is also represented at the **Wanda Gag House.** Children's author Wanda Gag, author and illustrator of such classics as *Millions of Cats,* was born and raised in this home in New Ulm. The compact home with turrets and skylights makes for an interesting afternoon's exploration.

For an oasis in the city, visit **Flandrau State Park.** At only 800 acres, this is a smaller park, but popular nonetheless, due in no small part to the fact that it's within walking distance from downtown New Ulm. The sand-bottomed swimming pond and extensive campgrounds are a big draw here, as are the hiking trails. The trails are groomed for cross-country skiing in the winter, and ski and snowshoe rentals are available.

Beer is not the only adult beverage produced in the New Ulm area. Take MN 68 to CR 47 south, then 101 south. The first farm on the left is **Morgan Creek Vineyards,** part of the **Three Rivers Wine Trail.** Morgan Creek is the only Minnesota vineyard with an underground winery. Stop by during their regular business hours for tours and tastings, or check their website for one of the numerous special events.

As befits a historic river town, New Ulm has several lovely bed & breakfasts available for lodging, many of which are more than one hundred years old. Good choices include the **Deutsche Strasse,** the **Beyer Haus,** the **Bohemian,** and **Bingham Hall.**

There are several choices for dining. For a meal reflecting the town's heritage, stop by the **Kaiserhoff,** New Ulm's oldest German restaurant, and try the ribs. **George's Fine Steaks and Spirits** is a congenial steakhouse in a pretty bistro building, and one of the best choices for a more upscale meal. If cozy and casual is what you're looking for, check out the **Ulmer Café,** the local diner with plentiful breakfasts and lunches. Another good choice is the **Backerei and Coffee Shop,** a longtime local bakery that still knows how to produce the pastries, and the prices are very reasonable.

Shopping options abound, and there are retailers that reflect New Ulm's German heritage. **Domeier's German Store** is packed full of German imports from the kitschy to the classic to the collector's dreams. The **Guten Tag Haus** is an importer of German gifts, including a large array of Christmas items. The **Sausage Shop** sells all kinds of meats—especially sausage—and baked goods too.

Other shops considered browse-worthy are **Weeds & Reeds,** a fun home-and-garden gift store built into a renovated 1926 gas station. Those searching for antiques need to stop by **Antiques Plus,** which houses more than 25 antiques dealers selling a wide variety of items.

## IN THE AREA

### Accommodations

**Beyer Haus Bed & Breakfast,** 224 South Broadway, New Ulm. Call 507-354-3180. Website: www.beyerhaus.com.

**Bingham Hall Bed & Breakfast,** 500 South German Street, New Ulm. Call 507-354-6766. Website: www.bingham-hall.com.

**The Bohemian Bed & Breakfast,** 304 South German Street, New Ulm. Call 507-354-2268. Website: www.the-bohemian.com.

**Deutsche Strasse Bed & Breakfast,** 404 South German Street, New Ulm. Call 507-354-2005; 866-226-9856. Website: www.deutschestrasse.com.

### Attractions and Recreation

**August Schell Brewery,** Schell's Road, New Ulm. Call 507-354-5528. Website: www.schellsbrewery.com.

**Brown County Historical Museum,** 2 North Broadway Street, New Ulm. Call 507-233-2616. Website: www.browncountyhistorymnusa.org.

**Fairfax Historical Depot Museum,** 200 Park Street South, Fairfax. Call 507-426-7919. Website: http://fairfax.govoffice.com.

**Fairridge Trail,** Fairfax. Website: http://fairfax.govoffice.com.

**Flandrau State Park,** 1300 Summit Avenue, New Ulm. Call 507-233-9800. Website: www.dnr.state.mn.us/state_parks/flandrau/index.html.

*The gardens at Schell's Brewery, New Ulm.*

**Fort Ridgely State Park,** 72158 CR 30, Fairfax. Call 507-426-7840. Website: www.dnr.state.mn.us/state_parks/fort_ridgely/index.html.

**Glockenspiel,** Minnesota St. and 4th Street North, New Ulm.

**Harkin Store,** CR 21, New Ulm. Call 507-354-8666. Website: www.mnhs.org/places/sites/hs/.

**Heritage Tree,** 101 South Minnesota Street, New Ulm.

**Hermann Monument,** Center Street and Monument Street, New Ulm. Website: www.hermannmonument.com.

**John Lind House,** 622 Center Street, New Ulm. Call 507-354-8802. Website: www.thelindhouse.com.

**Morgan Creek Vineyards,** 23707 478th Avenue, New Ulm. Call 507-947-3547. Website: www.morgancreekvineyards.com.

**Wanda Gag House,** 226 North Washington Street, New Ulm. Call 507-359-2632. Website: www.wandagaghouse.org.

**Way of the Cross,** 1500 Fifth North, New Ulm.

## Dining

**Backerei and Coffee Shop,** 27 South Minnesota Street. Call 507-354-6011. Open daily for breakfast.

**George's Fine Steaks and Spirits,** 301 North Minnesota Street, New Ulm. Call 507-354-7440. Open daily for lunch and dinner. Congenial steakhouse in a pretty bistro building. Website: www.georgessteaks.biz.

**Kaiserhoff,** 221 North Minnesota Street. Call 507-359-2071. Open daily for lunch and dinner.

**Lola's Larkspur Market,** 16 North Minnesota Street, New Ulm. Call 507-359-2500. Open Mon. through Sat. for lunch, Thurs. through Sat. for dinner. Hearty sandwiches and pasta dishes. When the weather is good, head for the patio. Website: www.lolaslarkspurmarket.com.

*Wanda Gag House, New Ulm.*

**Plaza Garibaldi,** 1707 North Broadway, New Ulm. Call 507-359-7073. It might seem odd to choose Mexican food in such a richly German community, but the menu offerings, both authentic and more Americanized, are worth the visit. Website: www.plazagaribaldinewulm.com.

**Ulmer Café,** 115 North Minnesota Street. Call 507-354-8122. Open daily for breakfast and lunch.

## Other Contacts

**City of Fairfax,** 112 1st Street SE, Fairfax. Call 507-426-7255. Website: http://fairfax.govoffice.com.

**New Ulm Convention & Visitors Bureau,** 1 North Minnesota Street, New Ulm. Call 888-463-9856. Website: www.newulm.com.

*Overlook at Eagle Bluff Environmental Learning Center.*

CHAPTER

14

# River Bluffs and Amish Country

**Estimated length:** 80 miles
**Estimated time:** 2.5 hours minimum

**Getting there:** From the Twin Cities or Rochester, take US 52 south to Preston.

**Highlights:** Visit the Root River Valley towns of Preston and Lanesboro; shop in the Amish town of Harmony; explore the Root River Trail; tour Amish Country. This is a great area for fall colors.

This stretch of southeastern Minnesota along the Iowa border is unlike many of its northern counterparts in that its dramatic topography is not the direct result of the last round glaciers (the Wisconsin glaciation from about 75,000 years ago) driving through centuries ago. Instead the geologic area is referred to as driftless, with spots of karst topography—an area, in this case, built of limestone and characterized by caves and sinkholes. That's good news for travelers interested in caving and for those who want to soak in dramatic scenery. While this is an easy day trip from the Twin Cities, many people make a weekend of it in order to have plenty of time to explore. Note: plan well in advance if you want to book one of the area's popular bed & breakfasts for summer and fall weekend visits—they can book up months ahead, and there's little in the line of traditional hotels to handle drop-in visitors.

The town of **Fountain** is the gateway to the Root River bluff country, and it's the starting point for the **Root River Trail.** This 60-mile paved trail winds eastward, along the Root River and through rolling landscapes that include 300-foot-high bluffs, concluding in Houston, not far from the Wisconsin border. The scenery is spectacular, and offers both level trails (along a former railroad grade) and more challenging inclines that lead to gorgeous vistas. Those adventurous enough to bike the entire trail will be rewarded with changing scenery that includes wooded areas, rivers and bluffs, and an attractive array of wildlife. The trails are open for cross-country skiers in the winter (seasonal fees apply). You can kick off your stop here with lunch at **Los Gables,** an authentic Mexican restaurant where you'd least expect it.

The trail first travels south to the town of **Preston,** which is the county seat. Like many of the small towns in this region, Preston was built in the mid-1800s, taking advantage of the proximity to the Root River to establish traffic corridors for milling operations. Preston is a crossroads of sorts, with the Root River Trail continuing northeast and a second branch, the **Harmony-Preston Valley Trail,** extending south to the Amish community of **Harmony.** Preston is also on the **Historic Bluff Country National Scenic Byway,** an 88-mile stretch of MN 16 that runs from **La Crescent** in the east to **Dexter** in the west, covering miles of rivers, bluffs, sprawling farmland, and miles of forests, including the **Richard J. Dorer Memorial Hardwood State Forest.** The Historic Bluff Country National Scenic Byway is dotted with small towns, many of which were built during the milling boom years. None of these towns has more than three thousand residents, and most have done an exemplary job of maintaining the buildings and natural environs, giving the Byway a feeling of visiting a time long gone. The presence of acres of deciduous trees, including several varieties of maples, elms, and birches, gives this area spectacular spring and fall views.

You can overnight in Preston at the **Jailhouse Inn,** the former county jail and sheriff's residence. Ten themed rooms pay homage to the inn's past, including the Drunk Tank and the Cell Block (and, in an odd twist, the Amish room). Before you set off to explore the bluff country, you can stop at the **Old Barn Resort** to play a round of golf riverside, followed by a hearty meal at the restaurant. Old Barn also has campsites available and hostel accommodations as well.

West of Preston is **Forestville/Mystery Cave State Park.** This state park has something for everyone: Mystery Cave takes visitors to underground pools and geologic cave formations; aboveground, hikers and horse riders have 15 miles of trails that wind through the bluff areas and through wild-flowers (in the spring). Skiers and snowmobilers are welcome in winter. Forestville is a trip back in time, to a once-functioning town that declined after the railroad bypassed it. Today visitors cross the Carnegie Steel Bridge to visit the General Store, where costumed guides lead tours and demon-strate activities from the store's late-1800s roots, and give tourists the chance to work with the farm laborers in the garden.

At this point, you can deviate slightly by traveling south on US 52 to **Harmony.** This, of course, is the other end of the Harmony-Preston Valley Trail. It's also the center point for the Amish community in Minnesota, with Amish farms and businesses surrounding it. Consequently, it's not unusual to see the black Amish buggies on the roads, so drive with extra caution. The stretch of US 52 between Preston and Prosper (southeast of Harmony) is known as the **Amish Buggy Byway,** and the highway has widened shoulders for use by the buggies.

The area's geologic forms are explained and on display at the **Harmony Area Historical Society,** which has exhibits about the karst topography and a new interpretive site on the topic of sinkholes. The karst is also responsible for a popular attraction: **Niagara Cave.** A one-hour guided tour is available; bring a jacket to fully enjoy the 60-foot underground waterfall and crystal wedding chapel.

Stop by **Slim's Woodcarving Museum,** the largest such museum in the United States, with over four thousand wood carvings on display, owned by artist Stanley "Slim" Maroushek. For more of Slim's work, check out the **Hobo Camp** at **Trailhead Park.** Life-size carvings of hobos are dis-played along with interpretive signage explaining the history and talents of hobos. **Austin's Mohair** will put you face to face with angora goats (espe-cially cute in the spring) and give you the opportunity to shop for mohair products, everything from yarn to clothing to goat milk soap.

There are several restaurants serving home-style meals. **Harmony House** serves breakfast and lunch, comprised of large omelets, cinnamon rolls, burgers, sandwiches, and a daily lunch special with mashed potatoes (not out of a box). **On the Crunchy Side** has a typical restaurant menu of steaks, pizzas, salads, burgers, and sandwiches. **QUARTER/quarter** is a more gourmet offering, with Caribbean and Santa Fe flavorings. **Village Square of Harmony** is the quintessential family restaurant, with a cheery red-and-white awning and a menu packed with pizza and sandwiches.

Amish goods and antiques figure heavily in the retail landscape. The **Amish Connection** and the **Village Depot and School** specialize in Amish goods, including furniture and quilts, while a wide variety of antiques can be found at **ANN-tiques and Collectibles, I Love Antiques, Old Crow Antiques,** and the **Generations of Harmony Antique Mall.**

Lodging choices are surprisingly diverse here. **Asahi Loft** has a distinctly Japanese feel to it, thanks to the years the owners spent in Japan and the decorating sensibility they brought back with them. **Selvig House,** built in 1910, is a more traditional bed & breakfast offering. **The Little House** is exactly what it says—a tiny but comfortable one-bedroom guesthouse. **Country Lodge Inn** is one of the few traditional hotel-style lodgings in the area, but still small with only 25 rooms.

Following MN 16 east will bring you to **Lanesboro.** Preston may be the county seat, but Lanesboro is tourism headquarters for the bluff country. The town itself is a gem, set gently into a valley with soaring bluffs along its northern edges. Lanesboro began as a resort town, with a dam built to create a lake, but its proximity to the Root River made it attractive for mill owners. The natural beauty of the area drew residents and farmers, includ-

*Lanesboro.*

ing a doctor whose avocation of bird-watching left behind highly detailed records still in use today. Red-shouldered hawks, bald eagles, wild turkeys, screech owls, and the tufted titmouse are just a few of the more than three hundred types of birds that have been identified around bluff country. To learn more about the birds in the area, and to find high-quality bird feed to take home, stop by **Avian Acres.**

Besides the Root River and Harmony-Preston Valley Trails, one of the best ways to explore nature is to spend time at the **Eagle Bluff Environmental Learning Center,** one of only seven such centers in the state and the only one south of the Twin Cities. Eagle Bluff has 80 acres of land surrounded by 1,000 acres of state forest, with hiking trails winding throughout and a scenic overlook from the top of a bluff over a deeply forested valley. The center offers residential programs for kids, adults, and families, including a challenging but popular ropes course. Course offerings run the gamut from canoeing to hiking, to learning to make maple syrup, to stargazing, to the basics of ecosystems and archery, fishing, orienteering, geocaching, and compass training.

Of course, you can manage your outdoor adventures yourself by bringing your transportation mode of choice with you. But if that's not practical, Lanesboro has several outfitters that can rent canoes, kayaks, inner tubes, and bikes. **Root River Outfitters** rents all of the above, and offers guided fishing trips. **River Rats Outfitters** rents canoes and kayaks, and owner Ken Soiney is a native of the area, so you can expect him to answer your questions, especially related to fishing and camping. **Little River General Store** provides canoes, kayaks, and bikes, and it also has a bike repair service if you've brought your own and run into trouble. All outfitters can arrange shuttle service.

Although easily explored on a day trip, Lanesboro is a popular overnight or long weekend destination, and with good reason. Besides biking, hiking, canoeing, kayaking, and tubing, the town of Lanesboro has plenty to offer. Drive down Parkway Avenue, Lanesboro's main street, and visit the business district, which is listed on the National Register of Historic Places. The northern end of the town ends with steep wooded bluffs, and the business district begins there. Lovingly restored Victorian storefronts feature shopping opportunities; **Olivia's Attic** stands out as a not-very-touristy shop with intriguing jewelry and art pieces, along with Amish furniture, and not a single tacky T-shirt to be found. Down the street is **Frank Wright, Spoonmaker,** a shop open limited hours but worth

## GUIDED TOURS

Along the Minnesota–Iowa border is a small but thriving Amish community, and there are tour companies who offer rides through the beautiful area as well as stops at selected farms and shops. Amish country tours operate Monday through Saturday in-season. For religious reasons, tours aren't available on Sunday. If you'd like to take photographs of Amish farms and buggies, that's fine, but please respect the beliefs of some orders of Amish that prohibit taking photos of people (based on the Second Commandment about not making graven images).

Amish Tours of Harmony offers tours Monday through Saturday, April through November. Discounts are given if you use your own vehicle. Flaby's Amish Tours operates Monday through Saturday, May through October. If you'd prefer a self-directed tour, an audio CD called *Amish Backroads Tour* is available from several Lanesboro retailers.

Lanesboro Trolley Tours offers a one-hour tour of the history and natural sights in Lanesboro itself.

Bluff Country Jeep Tours has daily tours (weather permitting) from April through October. For a more adventurous ride, try this tour, which goes over rough terrain and up into the hills and bluffs overlooking the river. Tours last one hour; think hard if you get carsick easily.

seeking out for Wright's unique sculptural spoons and other kitchen items. **Slant Avenue Mercantile,** so named for its precarious perch on a steep side street, is your source for tongue-in-cheek souvenirs, local artwork, and home decor. **Windy Mesa Jewelry and Art** showcases Navajo, Hopi, and Zuni art.

The arts community is alive and well in Lanesboro too. **Commonweal Theatre** (see sidebar) is a pillar of the community, supporting not only their own work but the efforts of nearby **Lanesboro Art Center.** The art center arranges exhibitions and juried gallery sales of local artists, as well as an annual Art in the Park event. They also arrange events and concerts at the **St. Mane Theatre.**

Dining in Lanesboro is a casual affair. That doesn't mean you can't find a gourmet meal—it just means you can dress casually and stay relaxed. If you want imaginative menus with locally sourced foods featured in seasonal dishes, try the **Old Village Hall Restaurant & Pub,** which might serve grilled beef filet with tarragon butter and horseradish mashed potatoes or salt cod cakes on black pepper biscuits with roasted pepper remoulade. Next door to the Commonweal is **Kari's,** which has somewhat erratic hours (be sure to check before planning a trip there) and serves Scandinavian gourmet food, like Norwegian meatballs with lingonberries and a variety of smørrebrøds. For more standard supper club fare, try **Riverside at the Root,** which has an excellent patio and serves up steak and pasta dishes. Dropping the price points down a bit, stop by the **Pedal Pushers' Café,** open for all three meals and using local sources for

*Frank Wright's Spoonmaker shop, Lanesboro.*

their burgers and chicken sandwiches, as well as serving homemade pie. Next door is **Das Wurst Haus,** open for lunch with homemade sausages and brats. In the residential area, the **Chat N Chew** is a reliable source for inexpensive, filling breakfasts and lunches.

If you've succumbed to the lure of Lanesboro and want to stay longer, there are several options. Keep in mind that most of the lodgings locally are small bed & breakfasts that, while lovely, are not always kid friendly and have limited rooms available.

There's a cluster of Victorian homes serving as bed & breakfasts in the southern end of Lanesboro. On Parkway Avenue South you'll find the **1898 Inn, Historic Scanlan House, O'Leary's,** and the **Victorian House.** Running parallel to Parkway is Fillmore Avenue, home to **Anna V's, Fillmore House,** and **Habberstad House.**

In the business district, check out the **Stone Mill Suites,** reconstructed from a former mill, or the **Cottage House Inn.** Nearby is **Belle Rive,** which accepts only one set of guests at a time.

Just a few miles outside Lanesboro are two beautiful and scenic lodging choices. **The Inn at Sacred Clay Farm** is surrounded by forests and long, sloping lawns, and has a two-story wraparound porch. It's also just down the road from the **Lanesboro State Fish Hatchery,** which periodically

---

## NATIONALLY KNOWN COMMONWEAL THEATRE

The **Commonweal Theatre** opened its doors in 1989, then again in 2007 in a
new building that allowed for larger audiences and more theatrical flexibility. It's
tempting to think of it as a tourist attraction, but with a season running from
April through December, the theater depends on local audiences as well. It's
nationally known for its expertise in the works of Henrik Ibsen and produces an
annual Ibsen Festival. The festival has received international acclaim, as well as a
grant from the Norwegian government to continue exploring Ibsen's work.
Besides Ibsen, Commonweal produces at least four other plays each year, sponsors readings of new works, and produces a live radio show every summer. The
new building's lobby was decorated by a local artist, who made creative use of
local artwork and artifacts that makes it worth a visit.

---

offers group tours. On a hillside overlooking miles of trees and farmland
is **Berwood Hill Inn,** which provides not only charming Victorian rooms,
but Adirondack chairs on the hillside to spend time admiring the view.

While a few of these places accept children, most don't. Four miles outside Lanesboro on County Route 16 (CR 16) is **Whalan,** a small town on
the Root River Trail. Here you'll find the **Cedar Valley Resort,** comprised of
several large log cabins perfectly designed for families, with volleyball and
horseshoe courts, fire pits, and lawn swings, and just steps from the trail.
Canoes, kayaks, and bikes are available for rent. On the other side of Whalan but also right on the trail is the **Cyclin-Inn,** a three-bedroom whole-
house rental. It's also conveniently located on the grounds of the **Gator
Greens Mini Golf.** Note: besides enjoying a few holes of mini golf, if you're
there at the right time of the summer you can also take advantage of pick-
your-own produce, including strawberries. Whalan is also home to a well-
loved local institution: the **Aroma Pie Shop.** The name says it all, and the
pies are made from scratch on-site. Lunch foods are also available.

Head south out of Whalan on CR 23 onto a gravel road that winds
through dense tree cover, and you'll suddenly turn a corner and find the
**Old Gribben Mill.** The remnants of a former milling operation, now
deserted, its stone construction crumbling, and with greenery growing over
it, will make you think you're somewhere in Europe instead of southern
Minnesota. Take a walk around the ruins (good shoes and long pants are
recommended, especially during tick season), or even a picnic basket. If

you explore back behind the ruins, you'll find seeping waterfalls near the bluffs.

Continuing east on CR 16 from Whalan brings you to the community of **Peterson,** which has two bed & breakfasts near the Root River Trail that are worth a visit: **Crossing Bed and Breakfast** and **Root River Inn.** Both are near a mill operation, which isn't as scenic as some of the Lanesboro properties, but the inns themselves are more than comfortable and literally only steps from the trail.

Further east is **Rushford,** where you can not only sample some of the Scandinavian delicacy known as *lefse,* you can learn how it's made (hint: rolling pins are crucial) at **Norsland Lefse.** Sweets of another kind are sold at the **Creamery,** which has 36 flavors of ice cream. Take your cone next door to **Nordic Lanes** if the weather isn't cooperating and bowl a few frames. When the weather improves, enjoy a little golf at the nine-hole

*Berwood Hill Inn.*

*Root River Inn, Peterson.*

**Ferndale Golf Course.** Younger travelers will definitely want to visit **Creekside Park,** an elaborate playground park built in 2009 to replace an older one destroyed by flooding in 2008. The bed & breakfast of choice here is **Meadows Inn,** recently built and lavishly appointed.

Before continuing east, take a detour south on MN 43 to **Choice,** home of a unique land formation known as **Cabbage Rocks,** an outcropping of rocks that strongly resemble heads of cabbage.

The last eastward leg of the trip heads back to MN 16 and on to Houston. Here you can get up close and personal with a buffalo at **Money Creek Buffalo Ranch** (and you can stay overnight at the ranch, in its rustic three-story log cabin). If you'd prefer something a little less rustic, reserve a room at the **Lilacs and Lace Guest House,** and enjoy the front-porch view of a neighboring park. While visiting, plan on taking a hike at **South Park,** which has trails that wind their way through valleys and up bluffs, where you will find striking rock formations.

Take MN 76 south out of Houston to find **Schech's Mill,** and tour the only remaining water-powered flour mill still operating in Minnesota. The milling history of this region is deep-rooted, and the opportunity to see it in action is well worth the time.

## IN THE AREA

### Accommodations

**The 1898 Inn,** 706 Parkway Avenue South, Lanesboro. Call 507-467-3539. One of a cluster of historic bed & breakfasts just blocks from Lanesboro's business district, this renovated Queen Anne home has two guest rooms, each with private bath. Breakfast is a special event, with home-baked breads and local, organic eggs and produce. Website: www.1898inn.com.

**Anna V's Bed and Breakfast,** 507 Fillmore Avenue South, Lanesboro. Call 507-467-2686. Another of the Victorian clusters on the south end of Lanesboro, this property has three guest rooms with private bath and full multicourse breakfast each day. Website: www.annavbb.com.

**Belle Rive Bed and Breakfast,** 302 Ashburn, Lanesboro. Call 507-467-2407. One set of guests at a time sets this bed & breakfast apart from the others in the heart of Lanesboro, as well as its patio overlooking the river. Website: www.bellerivebandblanesboro.com.

**Berwood Hill Inn,** 22139 Hickory Road, Lanesboro. Call 800-803-6748. Five miles from downtown Lanesboro is possibly one of the most romantic inns in the area. Built in the late 1800s, the Berwood Hill Inn sits high on a hill, overlooking miles of farmland and forested valleys. Website: www.berwood.com.

**Cedar Valley Resort,** 905 Bench Street, Whalan. Call 507-467-9000. This family-friendly resort, just steps from the Root River Trail and along the Root River, offers large cabins suitable for large families or family reunions. Canoes, kayaks, inner tubes, and cross country skis are available for rent on-site. Website: www.cedarvalleyresort.com.

**Cyclin-Inn,** 439 Half Street, Whalan. Call 507-251-5101. A few yards from the Root River Trail and next to Gators Greens Mini Golf is this whole-house rental, with three bedrooms and fully stocked kitchen.

During the summer, pick your own produce (for a fee) for your meals. Website: www.cyclin-inn.com.

**Habberstad House,** 706 Fillmore Avenue South, Lanesboro. Call 507-467-3560. Six beautiful rooms and suites are tucked inside a faithfully restored Victorian home, surrounded by lush gardens and sitting areas. Website: www.habberstadhouse.com.

**Historic Scanlan House B&B,** 708 Parkway Avenue South, Lanesboro. Call 800-944-2158. This striking 1889 Queen Anne mansion has seven elaborately furnished and romantic rooms and suites, all with private bath. The home itself is packed with antiques, and beds and windows are dressed in linens and lace. Website: www.scanlanhouse.com.

**Inn at Sacred Clay Farm,** 23234 Grosbeak Road, Lanesboro. Call 866-326-9600. Set on 100 acres just 3 miles outside downtown Lanesboro, the Inn at Sacred Clay Farm is a post-and-beam building with five rooms and suites, as well as meeting space. Large wraparound porches afford ample views of the countryside. Children ages eight and older are welcome. Note: rooms do not have TVs, phones, or computer access.

**Jailhouse Inn,** 109 Houston Street Northwest, Preston. Call 507-765-2181. Website: www.jailhouseinn.com.

**James A. Thompson House,** 401 Parkway Avenue South, Lanesboro. Call 507-467-2253. Overlooking the Root River with views from its rear porch, this bed & breakfast has four guest rooms. Website: www.jamesa thompsonhouse.com.

**Meadows Inn Bed and Breakfast,** 900 Pine Meadows Lane, Rushford. Call 507-864-2378. A large European-style building, the Meadows has five rooms with private baths, extensive gardens, and a sizable patio, and guests are welcome to explore and relax. Children allowed with parents. Website: www.meadowsinn.com.

**Mrs. B's Historic Lanesboro Inn,** 101 Parkway Avenue North, Lanesboro. Call 507-467-2154. A large and lovely limestone building on the Root River and right in downtown Lanesboro, Mrs. B's has nine rooms with private baths, warmly decorated with color and quilts. Feel brave? The inn continues to undergo studies by After Hours Paranormal Investigations. Website: 222.mrsbsinn.com.

**O'Leary's Bed and Breakfast,** 707 Parkway Avenue South, Lanesboro. Call 507-467-3737. Five rooms, all with private bath, located in the cluster of Victorian homes in south Lanesboro. Website: www.olearysbandb.com.

**Root River Inn,** 425 Prospect Street, Peterson. Call 507-875-2587. Nine rooms, all with private bath, are offered between the main house and the carriage house. Rooms are named for their color schemes, and all have period furniture and decor. The inn is a short walk from the Root River Trail. Breakfast served only on weekends. Website: www.wennesonhistoric inn.com.

**Scandinavian Inn,** 701 Kenilworth Avenue South, Lanesboro. Call 507-467-4500. The inn has five rooms with private bath, and it also has a rooftop gazebo and large front porch. Website: www.scandinavianinn.com.

**Stone Mill Suites,** 100 Beacon Street East, Lanesboro. Call 866-897-8663. This limestone mill served as both an egg and poultry processing plant and as a grain company from the time it was built in 1885. In 1999, the current owners bought it and created a B&B. Each of the ten rooms and suites is named and decorated after an aspect of the region, including the Amish Room, Grain Room, and the Egg Jacuzzi Suite. Unlike most bed & breakfast lodgings, kids are welcome here. Website: www.stone millsuites.com.

## Attractions and Recreation

**Amish Tours of Harmony,** Harmony. Apr. through Nov., Mon. through Sat., $20 adults, $6 children; free for ages three and under; discounts given if you use your own vehicle. Call 507-886-2303; 800-752-6474. Along the Minnesota–Iowa border is a small but thriving Amish community, and there are tour companies that offer rides through the beautiful area as well as stops at selected farms and shops. Website: www.amish-tours.com.

**Avian Acres,** CR 8, Lanesboro. Call 800-867-2473. Open Tues. through Sat. 9–6, occasionally on Mon. Website: www.avianacres.com.

**Bluff Country Jeep Tours,** Deep River Road, Lanesboro. Call 507-467-2415. Apr. through Oct. daily (weather permitting), $60 per ride (three people maximum).

**Commonweal Theatre,** 208 Parkway Avenue North, Lanesboro. Call 800-657-7025. Season runs Apr. through Dec. Website: www.commonweal theatre.org.

**Eagle Bluff Environmental Learning Center,** 28097 Goodview Drive, Lanesboro. Call 507-467-2437. Website: www.eagle-bluff.org.

**Flaby's Amish Tours,** Lanesboro. Call 507-467-2577; 800-944-0099. This company also offers Amish country tours, also with planned stops at farms and shops. May through Oct., Mon. through Sat. $20 adults, $6 children; free for ages three and under.

**Forestville/Mystery Cave State Park,** 21071 CR 118, Preston. Call 507-352-5111. Summer: open Sun. through Wed. 9–8, Thurs. through Sat. 9–9. Hours limited in winter months, call for information. Website: www.dnr.state.mn.us/state_parks/forestville_mystery_cave/index.html.

**Lanesboro Arts Center,** 103 Parkway Avenue North, Lanesboro. Call 507-467-2446. Open Tues. through Sun. 10–5, Mon. by appointment. Art gallery exhibiting and selling artwork by local and national artists. Website: www.lanesboroarts.org.

**Lanesboro Feed Mill,** 102 Beacon Street East, Lanesboro. Call 866-897-8663. Hours vary by business. Website: www.lanesborofeedmill.com.

**Niagara Cave,** 29842 CR 30, Harmony. Call 800-837-6606. Open Memorial Day through Labor Day daily, 9:30–5:30. Daily in May and Sept., weekends in Apr. and Oct., 10–4:30. Website: www.niagaracave.com.

**Old Barn Resort & Rivers' Bend Golf,** 24461 Heron Road, Preston. Call for hours. Website: www.barnresort.com.

**Root River and Harmony-Preston Valley Trails.** Website: www.rootriver trail.org.

**Scenic Valley Winery,** 103 Coffee Street East, Lanesboro. Call 507-259-4981. Open Apr. through Oct., Mon. through Sat. 10–5, Sun. 1–5. Call for appointment the rest of the year. Website: www.scenivvalleyresort.com.

**Stone House Trail Rides,** 21745 US 52, Preston. Call 507-765-4446. Open 9 AM–dark daily.

*The golf course at Old Barn Resort.*

## Dining

**Aroma Pie Shop,** 618 Main Street, Whalan. Call 507-467-2623. Open 10–5, Thurs. through Mon., May through Sept. Sandwiches, soups, hot dogs, brats—and of course, homemade pie.

**Branding Iron Supper Club,** 1100 Circle Heights Drive, Preston. Call (507) 765-3388. Open Tues. through Thurs. 11:30–8:30; Fri. through Sat. 11:30–9; Sun. 11–8:30. Closed Mon. Beautiful views from its hillside location and serving up some of the best steaks in the area. Website: http://brandingironmn.com/.

**Chat N Chew,** 701 Parkway Avenue South, Lanesboro. Call 507-467-3444. Open Mon. through Fri. 6–2; Sat. through Sun. 7–1:30; Fri. through Sat. 4–7. This small diner is a place to grab a quick sandwich or burger.

**Das Wurst Haus German Village & Deli,** 117 Parkway Avenue North, Lanesboro. Call 507-467-2902. Open daily 11–4, Apr. through Nov.

Generations-old family recipes are used to prepare the restaurant's meats, breads, desserts, and even the root beer. Stop by for lunch and enjoy your hearty sandwich or soup while listening to live polka music. An adjacent shop sells the meats, mustard, and cheese.

**Harmony House Restaurant,** 57 Main Avenue North, Harmony. Call 507-886-4612. Open daily 5 AM–1:30 PM. Home cooking with an Amish bent. Website: www.eatatharmonyhouse.com.

**Historic Highland Store & Café,** 22485 391st Avenue, Lanesboro. Call 507-467-3438. Open Sun. 8–3, Mon. through Fri. 7–3. A former general store turned café, the Highland serves breakfast all day and lunch specials, sourcing locally and organically when possible. Website: www.highland store.net.

**Kari's,** 210 Parkway Avenue North, Lanesboro. Call 507-467-3381. Open periodically for dinner; call or check website for specific days. A new addition to the Lanesboro dining scene, Kari's offers an upscale Scandinavian experience, including smørrebrøds, made with locally sourced foods in-season. Groups can reserve a private dining session. Website: www .karisinlanesboro.com.

**Los Gables,** US 52, Fountain. Call 507-268-1020. Open Sun. through Thurs. 6:30 AM–8:30 PM, Fri. through Sat. 6:30 AM–10 PM. Los Gables is owned and operated by the Gomez family, using family recipes on the menu. If you like heat, let them know—they'll up the spice quotient for you. Website: www.losgables.com.

**Old Village Hall Restaurant & Pub,** 111 Coffee Street, Lanesboro. Call 507-467-2962. Open Tues. through Thurs. 5–8, Fri. 5–9, Sat. 4:30–9, Sun. 4:30–8. The beautifully renovated former village hall and jail, on the National Register, offers a menu that changes seasonally and takes advantage of local, seasonal foods, including herbs from the restaurant's own herb garden. The creative menu might include items like lamb chops with couscous or salmon in curry sauce. Check out the outdoor patio in the summer. Website: www.oldvillagehall.com.

**Pedal Pushers Café,** 121 Parkway Avenue North, Lanesboro. Call 507-467-1050. Open daily 8–8. A '50s-style restaurant with hearty breakfasts, sandwiches and burgers for lunch, and comfort food like chicken pot pie and homemade meat loaf for dinner. Fountain treats and homemade pie round out the menu, which also has daily blue plate specials. Website: www.pedalpusherscafe.com.

**QUARTER/quarter,** 25 Center Street E, Harmony. Call 507-886-5500. Website: www.quarterquarter.com.

**River Trail Picnic Basket,** 100 Parkway Avenue North, Lanesboro. Call 507-467-3556. Open Apr. through Oct., Fri. through Sat. 8–5. Ice cream, coffee drinks, sandwiches.

**Riverside at the Root,** 109 Parkway Avenue South, Lanesboro. Call 507-467-3663. In summer open Mon. through Thurs. 4:30–10, Fri. through Sat. 11–10, Sun. 11–8. Call for fall hours. A casual restaurant located on the Root River, with a patio and deck that takes advantage of the location. Some standard steakhouse items are offered, such as steak, pork, and walleye, along with pizza and pasta, and occasionally game items (elk). Website: www.rootriveroutfitters.com.

## Other Contacts

**Historic Bluff Country.** Call 800-428-2030. Website: www.bluffcountry .com.

**Lanesboro Chamber of Commerce,** 100 Milwaukee Road, Lanesboro. Call 800-944-2670. Website: www.lanesboro.com.

**Root River Trail.** Website: www.rootrivertrail.org.

*Pioneer cabin at Shetek State Park.*

CHAPTER

15

# Pioneer Trails, Different Eras

**Estimated length:** 140 miles
**Estimated time:** 4 hours

**Getting there:** From the Twin Cities, take US 169 south to Henderson, where you'll pick up MN 19 west to Morton. Note: this trip could easily be combined with Chapter 13, the Minnesota River Valley, Part 2: Mankato to Fairfax.

**Highlights:** A journey through the history of both Native Americans and the pioneers who were sometimes at odds with them: the Birch Coulee and Loyal Indian Monuments; the Lower Sioux Agency; the Laura Ingalls Wilder Museum and the Ingalls Dugout, musts for any pioneer enthusiast; the Sod House on the Prairie in Sanborn; and the Jeffers Petroglyphs.

This somewhat circular trip serves the purpose of both introducing you to the prairie lands of southwest Minnesota (see Chapter 16, Prairie Country, for more of this area) and exploring various facets of Minnesota's Native American and pioneer history, which are entwined for better and for worse.

The landscape changes significantly over this trip. Beginning at the Minnesota River, with its rolling, wooded hills, you'll move onto more level terrain and wide-open spaces. There's still water to be found, and trees, but there's also the beauty of far horizons and miles of flowing farmland. While much of the original native prairie disappeared under agricultural plantings years ago, some patches remain, and efforts are being made elsewhere to restore land to its original state. When you find true prairie grasses and wildflowers, take the time to appreciate them (especially in midsummer, when the wildflowers are at their most colorful). Places like the **Jeffers Petroglyphs** offer hiking options through prairie fields, and it's well worth the extra time.

Note: many of the sites listed here have limited visiting hours, and some are open only in the summer. Check the site's website (listed at the end of this chapter) or call for current information.

The first stop is the **Birch Coulee Battlefield,** just north of Morton at the junction of County Route 2 (CR 2) and CR 8. One of the toughest battles of the U.S.–Dakota war took place here on September 2, 1862. This war has been described as the Minnesota Civil War, and it had devastating effects on both sides in terms of losses and cultural/psychological impact. Today the site is a restored prairie area, with trails leading to various notable points that have detailed interpretive signs. Returning to Morton and traveling east on MN 19, the **Birch Coulee and Loyal Indian Monuments** are in view. The Birch Coulee Monument was built in 1892 to honor the soldiers involved in the Birch Coulee battle, and the Loyal Indian Monument followed in 1899 to honor six Dakota who saved the lives of white settlers. **Lower Sioux Agency,** southeast of Morton on County Road 2, created in 1853 as an administrative center for the new Dakota reservation, has a history center focused on life around the time of the Dakota War, a war in which 20 people were killed and more were captured in an attempt to force the white settlers to abandon the Minnesota River Valley. The Lower Sioux Agency exhibits examine the causes of the war, and demonstrate other facets of life for the Sioux during this time period.

After visiting the Lower Sioux Agency, go west on CR 2 one mile, then turn south on CR 13 and travel about 4 miles to reach the **Gilfillan Estate.** The estate was built by Charles Duncan Gilfillan, who raised livestock for export to Great Britain and was very successful. His son eventually donated the home to the Redwood County Historical Society, and he funded construction of several buildings in the nearby city of Redwood Falls, including city offices and a library. The Gilfillan home itself is fully furnished with antiques, and you can choose between a tour just of the house or add on a tour of the farm as well.

Continue south on CR 13 until you turn right to head west on US 14, also known as Laura Ingalls Wilder Historic Highway. The highway stretches from Pepin, Wisconsin (home of *Little House in the Big Woods*) to De Smet, South Dakota (*By the Shores of Silver Lake*). When you reach Walnut Grove, you've arrived at the location of *On the Banks of Plum Creek*. The Ingalls family arrived in Walnut Grove in 1874 and stayed two years, then returned in 1877 for two more years. There are few actual traces of their lives there; a school Laura attended and a hotel she worked at still exist, but are private homes not open to the public. The **Laura Ingalls Wilder Museum** itself is a collection of vintage and re-created pioneer buildings, none of which has a direct association with Laura, but the main Depot Building has a collection of items including a number of pieces once owned by Laura, including a quilt she made and needlework supplies. Fans of the

*Laura Ingalls Wilder dugout on Plum Creek.*

TV show will also enjoy stopping here, as a room is devoted to memorabilia from the show, and in the summer cast members sometimes make public appearances. For hard-core history buffs, this may not be worth a stop, but if you like general pioneer history and/or have kids traveling with you, it's definitely worth a visit.

Just 1.5 miles north on CR 5, however, is an artifact more directly linked to the Ingalls family. Along the banks of Plum Creek is a dugout home where the Ingalls family lived from 1874 to 1876 before selling it after several crop failures and moving to Iowa. The family's ownership was discovered by the illustrator of Laura's books, Garth Williams, who informed the current owners of the historic nature of their property. Although the dugout itself is not much more than a hollow in the ground, it's surprisingly moving, especially when you look down to Plum Creek (you can also walk down to it and enjoy some time wading in it). The site is scenic, and picnic tables are available to make a pleasant stop.

There are a couple of dining options in Walnut Grove, including **Nellie's Café,** open daily for lunch and breakfast, and the **Walnut Grove Bar & Grill,** a supper-club type of restaurant open every day but Sunday for lunch and dinner.

Take CR 5 south back to US 14 and continue west to Tracy, where you can find lodging at the **Wilder Inn Motel** or the **Valentine Inn Bed & Breakfast.** From Tracy, head south on CR 38 toward Currie. Continue west on CR 37 to **Lake Shetek State Park.** Besides being a lovely park with a fishing pier (Lake Shetek is the largest lake in southwest Minnesota), swimming beach, 14 miles of hiking trails, and 6 miles of paved biking trails, Lake Shetek State Park is home to the Koch Cabin, built in 1857 and thought to be the oldest building in the county. There is also the Shetek Monument, which memorializes the 15 settlers who were killed in the Dakota Conflict of 1862.

From the park, take CR 37 east to CR 38 south into Currie to visit the **End-O-Line Railroad Park and Museum.** Among the many exhibits is a manually operated turntable, still functional and in its original location, that's on the National Register of Historic Places. Other sights include a restored 1875 steam locomotive, an interpretive center with a wide variety of memorabilia, and an exhibit about hobos, bums, and tramps. There are several historic buildings to visit, including an original general store, school, courthouse, and church buildings, and a Lakota teepee. Note: there's a paved bike trail that connects End-O-Line with Lake Shetek State Park.

To find another historical site related to the Dakota Conflict of 1862, travel south on CR 38 from Currie, then turn east on MN 30, which leads to CR 11. Travel north on 225th Avenue to the **Slaughter Slough WPA** (Waterfowl Production Area). The parking lot is near the corner of 225th Avenue and 161st Street. In the Slough is a monument paying tribute to three separate groups who were involved in and lost lives during the Dakota Conflict: the Dakota, the white settlers, and the Fool Soldiers, young Lakota men who negotiated for the release of captives and were later shunned by other Lakota for their work. The Slough is also a great location for bird- and wildlife watching.

Resume driving east on MN 30, heading for Jeffers. Past the little town of Jeffers itself, take US 71 north to CR 10. Turn east onto CR 10, then south on CR 2 to reach the **Jeffers Petroglyphs.** Thought to date from 3,000 B.C. to possibly as recently as the mid-1700s, the islands of rock that appear throughout the prairie grasses hold over two thousand Native American carvings. Two separate trails visit the glyphs, both starting at the visitors center, one only .5-mile roundtrip, the other slightly over a mile. Interpreters are available to explain the significance of the glyphs, which have a wide range of subject matter and meaning: humans, arrows, elk, buffalo, deer, and turtles are just some of the identifiable figures. The glyphs detail the history of the region and the people, identifying significant events and sacred ceremonies. Native Americans still come today for religious visits.

But it's not just the historic or spiritual aspects that make this a worthwhile visit. The landscape is striking: pink quartzite, prickly pear cactus, and dozens of wildflowers. The Jeffers site has areas of prairie that are original, a rarity, and just over half of all the prairie at the site is part of the first prairie re-creation to be done in the state. In the northern reaches, areas of buffalo rubs can be seen, where migrating bison would stop to rub their coats against the rocks, eventually leaving them with a glossy surface. Take some time after visiting the glyphs to admire the rest of the scenery and hike the full trails.

The best time to visit is either morning or late afternoon, when the sunlight is less likely to make the glyphs hard to read. But even in the middle of the day, there are glyphs that can be recognized, and the guides can work with mirrors to help you see the less defined designs.

Heading back to US 71 and traveling north, you'll come full circle to US 14. Travel east on 14 about 1 mile, until you see the sign for **Sod House on the Prairie.** A personal project of owner Stan McCone, Sod House is actually several sod buildings, constructed meticulously in the size and with the materials the original pioneers used to build their first homes. The replica home site includes a sod home, dugout, and log cabin; the "soddie" was built in the style of Laura Ingalls Wilder's day, with 2-foot-thick walls and lumber roof and floor, as opposed to the dugout, which has a dirt floor and roof. In previous years, the soddie was available as a bed & breakfast, but for now only tours are offered. There are pioneer costumes available for both kids and adults, and the area around the sod homes is undergoing restoration to prairie lands, with a short trail running throughout. They may not be original sod houses, but they're historically accurate (and were included in a History Channel documentary) and give visitors a strong sense of what living in one was like.

*Inside the Sod House, Sanborn.*

Finally, if your journeys through pioneer trails have left you hungry, continue east to **Springfield,** a city running alongside the Big Cottonwood River. The historic downtown is charming and walkable, and there are more dining choices here than in most of the other communities in the region. Casual dining can be had at the **Solar Drive-In,** or nicer fare in a sit-down restaurant is available at **Tommy's Central Street Steakhouse.** You can combine dining with bowling at the **Garage.**

## IN THE AREA

### Accommodations

Accommodations are open year-round unless otherwise noted.

**Valentine Inn Bed & Breakfast,** 385 Emory Street, Tracy. Call 507-629-3827. Four rooms, all with private bath, in this Victorian home that began its life as a hospital. Two rooms have walkout porches. Rates start at $85.

**Wilder Inn Motel,** 1000 Craig Avenue, Tracy. Call 507-629-3350. A small motel a few miles from Walnut Grove, basic in amenities but well cared for.

### Attractions and Recreation

**Birch Coulee and Loyal Indian Monuments,** MN 19, Morton.

**Birch Coulee Battlefield,** CR 2 and CR 18, Morton.

**End-O-Line Railroad Park & Museum,** 440 North Mill Street, Currie. Call 507-763-3708. Website: www.endoline.com.

**Gilfillan Estate,** CR 13 and 67, Morgan. Call 507-249-3451. Website: www.redwoodcountyhistoricalsociety.com.

**Ingalls Dugout,** CR 5, Walnut Grove. Website: www.walnutgrove.org.

**Jeffers Petroglyphs,** US 71, Jeffers. Call 507-628-5591. Website: http://jefferspetroglyphs.com/.

**Lake Shetek State Park,** 163 State Park Road, Currie. Call 507-763-3256. Website: www.dnr.state.mn.us/state_parks/lake_shetek/index.html.

*Laura Ingalls Wilder Museum, Walnut Grove.*

**Laura Ingalls Wilder Museum,** 330 8th Street, Walnut Grove. Call 507-859-2358. Website: www.walnutgrove.org.

**Lower Sioux History Center,** 32469 County Highway 2, Morton. Call 507-697-6321. Website: www.mnhs.org/places/sites/lsa/.

**Sod House on the Prairie,** 12598 Magnolia Avenue, Sanborn. Call 507-723-5138. Website: www.sodhouse.org/.

## Dining

**The Garage,** 3 North Cass Avenue, Springfield. Call 507-723-6000. Bowling alley with pizza, pasta, and burgers.

**Nellie's Café,** US 14, Walnut Grove. Call 507-859-2384. Open daily for breakfast and lunch, Mon. through Fri. for dinner. Diner fare.

**Solar Drive In,** 623 West Rock Street, Springfield. Call 507-723-9141. Burgers and sandwiches. Website: www.solardrive-in.com/.

**Tommy's Central Street Steakhouse,** 8 West Central Street, Springfield. Call 507-723-9191. Steak, ribs, chicken, and sandwiches.

**Walnut Grove Bar & Grill,** 651 Main Street, Walnut Grove. Call 507-859-2399. American cuisine.

## Other Contacts

**Springfield Chamber of Commerce,** 33 South Cass Avenue, Springfield. Call 507-723-3508. Website: www.springfieldmnchamber.org/.

**Tracy Chamber of Commerce,** 372 Morgan Street, Tracy. Call 507-629-4021. Website: www.tracymnchamber.com.

**Walnut Grove.** Website: www.walnutgrove.org.

*Pipestone's historic downtown.*

CHAPTER

16

# Prairie
# Country

**Estimated length:** 45 miles
**Estimated time:** 1.5 hours

**Getting there:** From Rochester, head south on US 52, then take I-90 west before following US 75 north to Luverne. From Mankato, take MN 60 south to west I-90, then US 75 north to Luverne.

**Highlights:** The quintessential small town of Luverne; Blue Mounds State Park with its swimming beach and hiking trails through prairie grasses; the historic town of Pipestone and the adjacent Pipestone National Monument; and the town (and wind power center) of Lake Benton.

When people think of Minnesota, the images that are most likely to come to mind are, of course, lakes and acres of forests. That's not an inaccurate portrayal, especially in the northeast and north-central parts of the state, but it's not the only scenery to be found.

Along the border between Minnesota and South Dakota, from the Iowa border north, is an area known as the Coteau des Prairie. It's the remnant of many glacial movements and retreats. The highest part of the Coteau in Minnesota is known as Buffalo Ridge, an area around **Lake Benton** and **Pipestone** with bedrock of shale, sandstone, and clay that have settled over Sioux quartzite before being covered with layers of glacial drift. As opposed to other parts of Minnesota that have dramatic hills and valleys covered with trees, the Coteau des Prairie has long, sloping hills that were once covered with tallgrass prairie. Today most of that natural prairie growth has given way to agricultural endeavors, with long stretches of soybean and cornfields.

However, in the farthest southwest, there are still some natural prairie areas remaining, or in the process of being cultivated again. It's a unique kind of beauty. As Minnesota poet and essayist Bill Holm said in his essay "Horizontal Grandeur": "A woods man looks at 20 miles of prairie and sees nothing but grass, but a prairie man looks at a square foot and sees a universe; ten or twenty flowers and grasses, heights, heads, colors, shades, configurations, bearded, rough, smooth, simple, elegant. When a cloud passes over the sun, colors shift, like a child's kaleidoscope." Taking the time to explore this part of the state, less traveled than other areas, is a richly rewarding experience full of natural beauty, wide-open skies, wildlife, rivers, Native American sites, and the slowly returning prairie.

Note: When making plans to visit, check ahead for restaurant open and close times. Many restaurants are closed on Sundays, and some are closed Mondays as well.

Shortly after you leave I-90 for US 75 north, the town of **Luverne** comes into view. This community of about 4,600 people is the county seat for Rock County. From a tourist's perspective, though, it's representative of what most people dream of when they envision small-town America: a walkable downtown with historic buildings, quiet residential streets with charming Victorian homes and cottages, and a pride of place and history. Perhaps its biggest claim to fame is being one of the four towns profiled in Ken Burns's landmark documentary *The War*. Several residents of Luverne, all World War II veterans, were interviewed for the documentary, including fighter pilot Quentin Aanenson, for whom the local airport is named. The community's respect for these veterans is on view at the **Rock County Veterans Memorial,** on the grounds of the beautiful **Rock County Courthouse.** The courthouse, built in 1888 of Sioux quartzite, is on the National Register of Historic Places.

More history is offered at the **Rock County Historical Society,** which is open limited hours in the summer for visitors to peruse its holdings. The building itself, a former Unitarian Church built in 1899, is worth a stop.

Nearby is the **Hinkly House,** another lovely Sioux quartzite building from 1892, originally built by the town's mayor. Also on the National Reg-

*The Hinkly House, Luverne.*

ister of Historic Places, the Hinkly House is open for tours selected hours in the summer, or by appointment off-season.

The downtown area of Luverne along Main Street is dotted with century-old buildings, many constructed of Sioux quartzite. Of particular note is the **Historic Palace Theater,** which has been showing movies since 1915. Recent renovations have modernized its operations, but with its large pipe organ still intact, it's as far from a modern multiplex as you can get. It was also the site of the premiere of Ken Burns's *The War.*

History and art intersect at the **Brandenburg Gallery,** housed at the **Rock County Veterans Memorial Building.** Internationally renowned *National Geographic* nature photographer Jim Brandenburg, a Luverne native, has a gallery of his works for viewing and for sale, with a focus on the prairie lands around Luverne. Brandenburg is also one of the founders of the **Brandenburg Prairie Foundation,** which works to restore and expand native prairie grasses and flowers. (Brandenburg also has a gallery in Ely; see Chapter 3, Western Boundary Waters, for more information.) You can visit the work in progress at the **Touch the Sky Prairie,** an 800-acre tract of pristine prairie land just outside Luverne. Take US 75 north 4 miles to County Route 20 (CR 20). Drive 3 miles west on CR 20, then turn right and drive 1 mile. At the T intersection is the prairie, and a parking area at the top of the hill to the west. Visitors are welcome to explore the area.

The next stop north out of Luverne is at **Blue Mounds State Park.** The park can be accessed by bike or foot, taking the **Blue Mounds Bike Trail** from Blue Mound Avenue in Luverne, or by taking US 75 north by car to CR 20 (the same road that travels to the Touch the Sky Prairie). Go west on CR 20 for 1 mile to the park entrance. This 1,800-acre park sits above surrounding farmland by virtue of a natural pedestal of Sioux quartzite.

*Prairie trail at Blue Mounds State Park.*

The Blue Mounds were named for the way they looked to westward-moving settlers; this stretch of rock 1,250 feet long that runs in an east–west direction, corresponding to the rising and setting of the sun, is thought to have been placed by early Dakota. Interesting fact about the rock: each year at the spring and autumn solstice, the sunrise happens right on the east end and the sunset right on the west end. Deer, coyote, numerous birds, and even bison live here and can be seen by visitors.

The park is an excellent place to immerse yourself in the loveliness of the prairie, especially midsummer, when the wildflowers are in full bloom. The 13 miles of hiking trails wander deep into the prairie, and in some of the lower stretches hikers will find themselves threading a narrow path surrounded by wildflowers nearly 6 feet tall on either side. Bikers have access to 2 miles of paved trails as well. Rock climbing is available, as is swimming and camping. Don't miss the bison viewing stand—the park is home to a herd of bison that peacefully roam within a large, fenced space.

The drive from Luverne to **Pipestone** along US 75 is a quiet one, full of rolling farmlands and prairie remnants. Pipestone, a town rich in Native American and quarrying history, is named after the red stone called pipestone, or catlinite after the artist and writer George Catlin, who visited the area first in 1836, sketching it and recording the local legends. The community was further memorialized by poet Henry Wadsworth Longfellow's "Song of Hiawatha," although Longfellow never actually traveled to Pipestone. The pipestone was, and still is, central to Native American ceremonial rites. They quarried it to create pipes, an activity recorded by Lewis and Clark in the early 1800s. (See the Pipestone National Monument sidebar for more details.)

Its downtown is so packed full of historic quartzite buildings that the entire Main Street area is listed on the National Register of Historic Places, one of the largest such districts in the state. An easy walk of about 12 blocks, mostly along **Main Street and North Hiawatha Avenue,** will take you past the towering stone buildings, each with its year of construction at the top, and sometimes the name of the original owner. The buildings are striking not just for their "days gone past" architecture, but because of the distinctive red stone used to build them. On East Main Street are a series of buildings with whimsical gargoyles carved above the entrances, carved by sculptor Leon Moore (hence the building's name: the Moore Block). At the junction of Main and Hiawatha is the **Historic Calumet Inn,** built in 1888 and still in operation as a hotel, restaurant, and bar. It's a good option for overnighting in the area; it's hard to beat getting up in the morning and stepping right out into the historic district. Be sure to take a stroll around the **Pipestone County Courthouse** and the **Carnegie Library.** The **Episcopal Church** nearby was built in 1892 and is one of the oldest churches still standing in Pipestone. Finally, a visit to the **Pipestone County Museum,** housed in the Old City Hall, gives you not only a look at the inside of one of the historic buildings, but also at the history of the area overall.

Just a few blocks east of the historic district is the **Concrete Water Tower** in a rest area near US 75. The 132-foot concrete structure was built in 1920 and served the city until 1976. It's one of very few concrete water towers still in existence, and is also on the National Register of Historic Places.

Across from the Pipestone National Monument entrance is **Fort Pipestone Trading Post and Museum.** This replica of a stockade from the 1862 Sioux uprising is a little on the kitschy side and more entertaining to kids than to adults in search of serious history. But if you have young ones with you and are willing to browse the souvenirs, it's not a bad stop.

As mentioned previously, the Historic Calumet Inn is a good choice for really soaking up the historic atmosphere of this town; otherwise you're in a motel on the highway. Dining at the Calumet is worth a stop too, but make some time to eat at the very popular Lange's Café and Bakery on US 75. Lange's earned national attention when *Roadfood* writers Jane and Michael Stern highlighted its sour cream raisin pie as a don't-miss dessert. (But the stuffed hash browns at breakfast are worth considering, too.)

Like many communities, Pipestone has several annual events, but one of the biggest is **Civil War Days,** which takes place each year in August. The festival includes Civil War reenactments, reconstructed military camps, visits from Abe and Mary Lincoln, and other historical events and activities.

You could end the drive in Pipestone and feel like you've seen a lot, but a quiet closing trip is just a few more miles north on US 75. **Lake Benton** is located on the shores of Lake Benton (appropriately enough) and is in the valley of the Buffalo Ridge. Around Lake Benton you'll see a number of wind turbines, which take advantage of the rolling prairie land, relatively unobstructed by forest, to collect and harness wind power. There are more than 70 of these turbines in operation, generating enough power to provide electricity to 125 homes. To learn more about the process, visit

## PIPESTONE NATIONAL MONUMENT

Just outside Pipestone is one of two national monuments in Minnesota (the other is Grand Portage National Monument in the northeast corner of the state). **Pipestone National Monument** is a significant historic and cultural site. The red pipestone, so-called because its primary use is to be carved into ceremonial pipe bowls, has been quarried by Native Americans since at least the 17th century, and the quarry is viewed as a sacred site. The pipes from this quarry were highly acclaimed across the United States, and the land that produced it was, for the most part, neutral territory for different tribes because of the symbolic power of the site.

Today, the only quarrying allowed is by Native Americans, a right they retained when they sold the land to the U.S. government in 1937. A comprehensive visitors center details the significance and history of the area, and there are locally made pipestone products in the gift shop. During the summer months, visitors can watch as quarrying takes place.

Take time to hike the Circle Trail, a .75-mile walk from the visitors center, which provides beautiful views of quartzite, native prairie grasses and wildflowers, and Winnewissa Falls and the Oracle, a naturally occurring stone "face" that Native Americans believed to be a sentient being. Also of interest at the monument's entrance are the large granite boulders known as Three Maidens. The boulders were once one massive boulder that landed at this spot thanks to glaciers; many legends have sprung up about their meaning today.

the **Heritage and Wind Power Learning Center.** The center, opened in 2001, offers changing exhibits that illustrate how the wind power is collected and how it's used.

It's not all about wind power, though; Lake Benton also has the highly active **Lake Benton Opera House,** offering a variety of Broadway musicals and seasonal and children's productions. The building itself was first opened in 1896 but fell into disuse and disrepair in the late 1950s. In 1970, a group of local residents launched a campaign to save and restore the building, a process that took nearly 30 years because of the efforts to restore rather than replace.

If you're looking for a cozy, romantic escape, the **Benton House Bed & Breakfast** is on the edge of town with three charming rooms. Just outside the city is the **Wooden Diamond Bed & Breakfast,** which doesn't have any

*Benton House Bed and Breakfast.*

Victorian charm—but its location on the shores of Lake Benton more than makes up for it. Dining runs heavily to supper club or bar fare; check out the **Knotty Pine Supper Club** (a few miles west of Lake Benton, near Elkton, South Dakota) or the **Country House** for hearty meals.

## IN THE AREA

### Accommodations

**Benton House Bed & Breakfast,** 211 West Benton Street, Lake Benton. Call 507-368-9484. Website: www.itctel.com/bentonhs.

**Historic Calumet Inn,** 104 West Main, Pipestone. Call 507-348-7651. Set in the heart of historic downtown Pipestone, the Calumet itself is a historic building with small but charming rooms, a restaurant and bar on-site, and access to a recreation center across the street. Website: www.calumetinn.com.

**Wooden Diamond Bed & Breakfast,** 1593 Shady Shore Drive, Lake Benton. Call 507-368-4305. Website: www.woodendiamond.com.

## Attractions and Recreation

**Blue Mounds State Park,** 1410 161st Street, Luverne. Call 507-283-1307. Website: www.dnr.state.mn.us/state_parks/blue_mounds/index.html.

**Brandenburg Gallery/Rock County Veterans Memorial Building,** 213 East Luverne Street, Luverne. Call 507-283-1884. Website: www.jim brandenburg.com.

**The Country House,** 405 East Benton Street, Lake Benton. Call 507-368-4223. American cuisine.

**Fort Pipestone Trading Post,** 104 Ninth Street NE, Pipestone. Call 507-825-4474.

**Heritage and Wind Power Learning Center,** 110 South Center Street, Lake Benton. Call 507-368-9577, ext. 6.

*Wind turbines near Pipestone.*

**Hinkly House,** 217 North Freeman, Luverne. Call 507-283-9476.

**Historic District,** Pipestone. Call 507-825-3316. Website: www.pipestone minnesota.com.

**Pipestone National Monument,** US 75, Pipestone. Call 507-825-5464. Website: www.nps.gov/pipe.

**Rock County Courthouse/Veterans Memorial,** 204 East Brown Street, Luverne.

**Rock County Historical Society,** 123 North Freeman, Luverne. Call 507-283-2122.

## Dining

**Glass House Restaurant,** 711 MN 23, Pipestone. Call 507-348-7651. Steakhouse menu, including seafood and chicken, and a Sunday smorgasbord.

**Historic Calumet Inn,** 104 West Main, Pipestone. Call 507-348-7651. American food, full bar. Website: www.calumetinn.com.

**Knotty Pine Supper Club,** 1014 County Highway 10, Elkton, South Dakota. Call 507-548-3781. American cuisine.

**Lange's Café and Bakery,** 110 8th Avenue SE, Pipestone. Call 507-825-4488. Open 24/7, serving home-cooked meals including the usual sandwiches and soups as well as some more inventive pastas and meat dishes. Be sure to have the pie for dessert.

## Other Contacts

**Lake Benton Chamber of Commerce,** Lake Benton. Website: www.itctel .com/lbenton.

**Luverne Area Chamber of Commerce,** 213 East Luverne Street, Luverne. Call 507-283-4061. Website: www.luvernechamber.com.

**Pipestone Chamber of Commerce,** US 75 and MN 23, Pipestone. Call 507-825-3316. Website: www.pipestoneminnesota.com.